THE ESSENTIAL POETS

Walt Whitman

BORN 31 MAY 1819
DIED 26 MARCH 1892

THE ESSENTIAL
WHITMAN

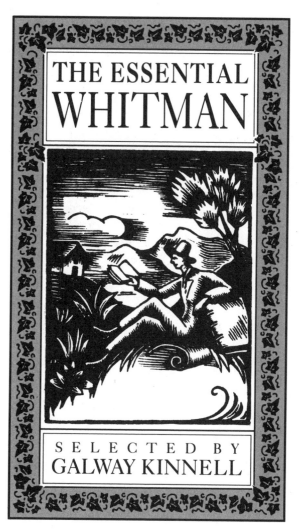

SELECTED BY
GALWAY KINNELL

GALAHAD BOOKS
NEW YORK

To Mary Kaplan

Published in 1992 by

Galahad Books
A division of LDAP, Inc.
386 Park Avenue South
New York, New York 10016

Galahad Books is a registered trademark of LDAP, Inc.

This edition published by arrangement with The Ecco Press

Library of Congress Catalog Card Number: 86-24075
ISBN: 0-88365-804-6

Original design by Reg Perry
Additional art and design for this edition by Cindy LaBreacht

Photograph of Whitman by G. Frank E. Pearsall, 1872
Reproduced by permission of the National Portrait Gallery,
Smithsonian Institute, Washington, D.C.; Gift of Mr. and Mrs. Feinberg

Printed in the United States of America

CONTENTS

THE ESSENTIAL
WHITMAN

INTRODUCTION

The poems of Walt Whitman meant little to me when I read them in high school and college. Luckily, when I was teaching at the University of Grenoble in my late twenties, I was required to give a course on Whitman. My experience of his work then was intense, the more so because, in a foreign country, it was my one real connection to my own language. Soon I understood that poetry could be transcendent, hymnlike, a cosmic song, and yet remain idolatrously attached to the creatures and things of our world. Under Whitman's spell I stopped writing in rhyme and meter and in rectangular stanzas and turned to long-lined, loosely cadenced verse; and at once I felt immensely liberated. Once again, as when I first began writing, it seemed it might be possible to say everything in poetry. Whitman has been my principal master ever since.

So the choice of poems for *The Essential Whitman* came naturally. I simply made a list of the poems I like best. I discovered that my list included the poems generally thought to be Whitman's greatest and that it represented the major aspects of his poetic talent. My selection did not differ much from the selection most modern editors would make. Only "The Runner" and "Sparkles from the Wheel" might be considered idiosyncratic choices. Wonderful poems were left out, but in such a book, this is as it must be; nor, regrettably, was there room for the lecture-essay, "An American Primer" or selections from *Specimen Days*.

Once I had settled upon which poems to use, all that remained to do was to choose the versions. This proved to be more difficult. *Leaves of Grass* came out in six editions. Each time Whitman added new poems,

enlarging the book from twelve poems in 1855 to 383 in 1892. He also revised the poems already present. Many of the revisions could be called fine tuning, but quite a number went to the very heart of the poems. A poem called "Great Are the Myths" in successive editions was revised, lengthened, shortened, and at last dropped. Whitman took passages from one poem and put them in another. He made several poems of one poem, one poem of several. "Song of Myself" did not reach final form until twenty-six years after first publication.

Normally, of course, an editor would present the poems in the versions the author considered final. And indeed, some of Whitman's changes improve the poems in important ways. His deletions, in particular, are often well taken and sometimes make a decisive difference. Here, for example, are three lines from the 1855 version of "Song of Myself":

> *Swiftly arose and spread around me the peace and joy and knowledge that*
> *pass all the art and argument of the earth;*
> *And I know that the hand of God is the elderhand of my own,*
> *And I know that the spirit of God is the eldest brother of my own*

Here are the lines again as they appear in 1881:

> *Swiftly arose and spread around me the peace and knowledge that pass all*
> *the argument of the earth,*
> *And I know that the hand of God is the promise of my own,*
> *And I know that the spirit of God is the brother of my own*

The substitution of "promise" for "elderhand" in the second line is, to me, an error, but the deletions in the first and third lines are brilliant. In the first instance, taking away a few nouns transforms one of Whitman's most cluttered lines into one of his most flowing and moving. When the unnecessary adjective is stricken from the third line, it, too, suddenly shines.

Not only deletions, but rewritings as well, occasionally improve the poems. How much more immediate "Crossing Brooklyn Ferry" became after Whitman rewrote the first line,

Flood-tide of the river, flow on! I watch you face to face,

to read:

Flood-tide below me! I see you face to face!

The 1856 line, "I too lived,"—weakened by the 1860 revision, "I too lived, (I was of old Brooklyn),"—came to perfection in 1867: "I too lived, Brooklyn of ample hills was mine."

If most of the changes were as good as these, the question of which version to use would not arise. An editor would simply reprint the poems as Whitman left them. But most readers who look closely at Whitman's revisions soon realize that while some may help, most do not, and many harm the poems, often severely. Whitman may be poetry's most spectacular victim of the law of elapsed time.

All writers know this law: revision succeeds in inverse ratio to the amount of time passed since the work was written. Revision is most likely to improve a poem when it directly follows composition, because it is, in fact, a slower, more reflective phase of the creative act. It is most likely to fail if many years have passed—such as the quarter century between the first publication and the last revision of *Leaves of Grass.* The only exception to the law is that ill-written and extraneous material may be excised with good effect at any time.

One reason why delayed revision often fails is that the writer eventually loses track of what he or she was originally trying to do—or more likely, was doing without trying. Great works are often written more by ex-

ploration, by feel, by instinct, than by fixed intention; and so it is easy for an author to forget the reasons — if he or she ever articulated them — for those inspired leaps, those sudden decisions and shifts of direction, which were vivid and compelling during composition. When Socrates questioned the poets of Athens, he discovered they wrote not by reason but by inspiration or madness and could not tell him what their poems meant. Certainly it was in an inspired, mad, illuminated state that Walt Whitman wrote the first version of *Leaves of Grass*. Sure enough, as Malcolm Cowley shows in the introduction to his reissue of the 1855 *Leaves of Grass*, before long Whitman forgot the original intent of his poem.

In particular, he forgot that the poem which was to become known as "Song of Myself" was not about himself, Walter Whitman, but about a representative man, a workman-poet, "Walt Whitman, an American, one of the roughs, a kosmos," as he describes himself in the 1855 edition, a person, furthermore, who was "not merely of the New World but of Africa Europe or Asia — a wandering savage." With each revision the poem became less representative and more exclusively autobiographical. In 1867 he changed the above description of the author to read, "Walt Whitman am I, of mighty Manhattan the son," and dropped the part about belonging to other continents. In 1881 he added this passage, suggesting that the protagonist is literally himself:

> *My tongue, every atom of my blood, form'd from this soil, this air,*
> *Born here of parents born here from parents the same, and their parents*
>   *the same,*
> *I, now thirty-seven years old in perfect health begin,*
> *Hoping to cease not till death.*

In 1860 Whitman scrapped the 1856 title, "A Poem of Walt Whitman, an American," which makes clear the representative character of the poet-hero, and in 1881 he called it, "Song of Myself," a title which allows one to think the poem is about the actual author.

Another reason for the law of elapsed time is that the poet who revises belatedly may no longer be exactly the same person who composed. Certainly Whitman was not. As the Good Gray Poet (a mantle he put on in the late 1860s), he had lost some of his youthful arrogance, intransigence, and extraordinary shamelessness. Perhaps, too, he had been chastened by Emerson's new aloofness, by mocking reviews, by the realization that over the years he was acquiring notoriety but not readers. He began to excise from poems things he had once blurted out that could expose him to ridicule. From "Crossing the Brooklyn Ferry," for example, he removed a reference to himself as a "solitary committer" (whatever that is, but it sounds awful) and he dropped some brilliant but revealing passages from "The Sleepers," including this mysterious evocation of adolescent experience:

> *I feel ashamed to go naked about the world.*
> *I am curious to know where my feet stand — and what is this flooding*
> *   me, childhood or manhood — and the hunger that crosses the bridge*
> *   between.*

> *The cloth laps a first sweet eating and drinking,*
> *Laps life-swelling yolks — laps ear of rose-corn, milky and just ripened;*
> *The white teeth stay, and the boss-tooth advances in darkness,*
> *And liquor is spilled on lips and bosoms by touching glasses, and the best*
> *   liquor afterward.*

He also dropped this tortured denunciation of his father:

> *Now Lucifer was not dead — or if he was I am his sorrowful terrible heir,*
> *I have been wronged — I am oppressed — I hate him that oppresses me,*
> *I will either destroy him, or he shall release me.*

> *Damn him! how he does defile me,*
> *How he informs against my brother and sister and takes pay for their*
> *   blood,*

How he laughs when I look down the bend after the steamboat that carries away my woman.

Now the vast dusk bulk that is the whale's bulk, it seems mine,
Warily, sportsman! though I lie so sleepy and sluggish, my tap is death.

The man who once said, "Unscrew the locks from the doors! Unscrew the doors themselves from their jambs!" apparently had second thoughts and wanted to screw the locks and doors back on again.

This self-protective, perhaps somewhat self-important new Whitman took on a more conventional poetic style as well. "Song of Myself" had started out to be a "language experiment": mixing the plain names of things, the great basic words, popular locutions, slang, technical terminology, disappeared words, Whitman proposed a new language for American poetry, contemporary, vivid, muscular, and at the same time fantastic, musical, and self-generating. But by the mid-sixties his work began to fill up with the very poeticisms and archaisms he had started off by excluding—"o'er," "e'en," "erewhile," "i'," " 'tis," "ope," and many more.* Whitman changed "listen" to "list" and eventually went so far as to title a poem, "On, on the Same, ye Jocund Twain!"

Many of Whitman's revisions seem intended to domesticate the "barbaric yawp" and make his verse sound more recognizably like poetry. He inverted word order: "Now I stand on this spot," became, "Now on this spot I stand"; "Out of the rocked cradle," turned into, "Out of the cradle endlessly rocking." Whitman went back over the whole text of *Leaves* and changed the preterite and past participle "ed" to " 'd" so that, on the page, in this respect at least, his work would look like the poetry of the past. He threw in more and more foreign words, some-

* For a fuller discussion and more illustrations, see Roger Asselineau, *The Evolution of Walt Whitman*, vol. II of *The Creation of a Book* (Cambridge, Mass.: Harvard University Press, 1962).

times with comic effect: "No dainty dulce affettuoso I!" His old, bold way of setting simple declarative sentences side by side must have struck him now as inelegant, and he subordinated one to the other: "He turns his quid of tobacco, his eyes get blurred with the manuscript," became, "He turns his quid of tobacco while his eyes blur with the manuscript."

He became less trustful of the common instinct that makes language intelligible and felt it necessary to explain perfectly comprehensible, spontaneous turns of phrase: "Sleeps at my side all night and close on the peep of the day," became, "Sleeps at my side through the night, and withdraws at the peep of the day with stealthy tread," and, "The suns I see and the suns I do not see," turned into the mostly redundant: "The bright suns I see and the dark suns I cannot see." Slightly odd constructions he conventionalized: "The worst suffering and restless," became, "The worst suffering and the most restless." He revised straightforward phrases to make them more literary and deleted some of his happiest, but unliterary, touches. The word that had to disappear from this line, "Where the laughing-gull scoots by the slappy shore and laughs her near-human laugh," is, of course, "slappy." And this wonderfully wacko line, "Washes and razors for foofoos—for me freckles and a bristling beard," he dropped entirely.

These examples of Whitman's destructive changes illustrate the hard choices facing an editor. The sad truth is that the final edition of *Leaves of Grass* is far less exciting than the first. Some of the great poems are muddy from too much tampering. Wonderful passages are missing. The original daring and verbal brilliance had been compromised. "Song of Myself" has changed its very character. Much as I believe in respecting a poet's own final judgment about his poems, I found it too painful to present *Leaves of Grass* in this form.

The obvious alternative, to follow Malcolm Cowley and give the poems in their original, most energetic versions, was very appealing. The drawback was that to do so would mean ignoring those occasional

brilliant rewritings that Whitman came up with, and leaving in place dull and superfluous lines that Whitman wisely struck out.

I puzzled long and hard over the dilemma—to use the latest versions and get some of the great poems in inferior form, or to present the earliest versions and do without the best of the revisions.

I came up with this solution. I took as my starting point what I regard as the most satisfactory version of each poem (usually, but not always, the earliest version). I then compared it with all other versions. When I found a distinctly superior reading—some happy rewriting or blessed deletion, or in the case of superseded versions, an abandoned felicity— I incorporated it into the version at hand. Some of the poems in this book, therefore, are in versions that have never existed before.

No doubt some readers will object to this procedure. They will not be mollified by knowing that the incorporations from other versions are rather few and that all of them are indicated in the notes. I understand the objection. My only justification is the hope that, unorthodox as it is, the method has made it possible to present Whitman's poetry at its best. And I know this method makes the book unsuitable for readers who, for whatever reason, need an intact version. Happily for them— and indeed for all who would judge the quality of Whitman's revisions for themselves—the editions of 1855, 1860, and 1881 are in print.

In punctuation I have usually followed the practice of the 1860 edition for poems published up to that time: dashes and commas, rather than a series of dots, to indicate caesuras; aversion to the exclamation point and semicolon; and a weakness for hyphenation. In later poems I have used the punctuation of the 1881 edition, except that I have kept all the original dashes and many of the discarded commas.

The first three editions of *Leaves of Grass* did not have numbered sections. In the fourth and fifth editions Whitman went back and divided

some of the longer poems into sections. The section divisions are so useful that I have put them into even the early, unsectioned versions. The reader will know a version did not have sections to begin with when the section numbers appear on the left-hand margin; and that they originally did have sections when the numbers are centered, in larger type face, above the sections.

As for titles, it would have been simple to use the familiar ones in the 1881 edition. In the case of four poems, however, I chose earlier titles. With one, I had no alternative. The later title, "I Sing the Body Electric," is the first line of the poem, but in the version used here ("Poem of the Body") it does not appear at all.

My choice of titles for the other three was more a matter of judgment. The 1860 title, "Sleep-Chasings," is more apt than "The Sleepers," since only a part of this poem concerns sleepers, whereas all of it can be characterized as "sleep-chasings." The 1856 title, "Poem of the Proposition of Nakedness," has the no-nonsense, let's-just-describe-the-poem quality of all the early titles, and I find it more satisfactory than the catchier, "Respondez!" "Elemental Drifts" is a title too beautiful in itself to exchange for "As I Ebbed with the Ocean of Life."

I kept the title "Song of Myself" even though it may not be quite as accurate as the earlier, "A Poem of Walt Whitman, an American." This latter I have appended as a subtitle, hoping it will discourage a narrowly autobiographical reading.

A word about "Once I Passed Through a Populous City," which appears here in the manuscript version. As published, the poem describes an encounter with a woman, but in this version, the encounter is with a man. To fit the poem in the "Enfans d'Adam" poems, that section of *Leaves of Grass* about love between a man and a woman, Whitman changed the man to a woman and deleted both the poignant "we wandered" and, what is so precious and so seldom found in love poems, the

evocation of the actual other—"one rude and ignorant man." I find the manuscript version stronger by far.

Whitman spent the last part of his life trying to get his book right. He kept working over those old poems, as Lady Gregory said of Yeats, as if he were in competition for eternity. As Whitman grew older, not only did his creative powers wane but his critical faculties became erratic, and he was never able to achieve that last goal and make a perfect *Leaves of Grass*. On the contrary, the more he searched for perfection, the further away it went. A year before his death, Whitman said, "In the long run the world will do what it pleases with the book." I would like to interpret this remark as indicating acceptance of such enterprises as this attempt of mine to consolidate the best of all his efforts to perfect his finest poems.

GALWAY KINNELL

 POEMS

Song of Myself: A Poem of Walt Whitman, an American

1

I celebrate myself,
And what I assume you shall assume,
For every atom belonging to me, as good belongs to you.

I loafe and invite my soul,
I lean and loafe at my ease, observing a spear of summer grass.

2

Houses and rooms are full of perfumes—the shelves are crowded with
    perfumes,
I breathe the fragrance myself, and know it and like it,
The distillation would intoxicate me also, but I shall not let it.

The atmosphere is not a perfume—it has no taste of the distillation,
    it is odorless,
It is for my mouth forever—I am in love with it,
I will go to the bank by the wood, and become undisguised and naked,
I am mad for it to be in contact with me.

The smoke of my own breath,
Echoes, ripples, and buzzed whispers, love-root, silk-thread, crotch
    and vine,
My respiration and inspiration, the beating of my heart, the passing of
    blood and air through my lungs,

The sniff of green leaves and dry leaves, and of the shore and dark-colored
    sea-rocks, and of hay in the barn,
The sound of the belched words of my voice, words loosed to the
    eddies of the wind,
A few light kisses, a few embraces, a reaching around of arms,
The play of shine and shade on the trees as the supple boughs wag,
The delight alone or in the rush of the streets, or along the fields
    and hillsides,
The feeling of health, the full-noon trill, the song of me rising from
    bed and meeting the sun.

Have you reckoned a thousand acres much? Have you reckoned the
    earth much?
Have you practiced so long to learn to read?
Have you felt so proud to get at the meaning of poems?

Stop this day and night with me and you shall possess the origin of
    all poems,
You shall possess the good of the earth and sun—there are millions
    of suns left,
You shall no longer take things at second or third hand, nor look
    through the eyes of the dead, nor feed on the spectres in books,
You shall not look through my eyes either, nor take things from me,
You shall listen to all sides and filter them from yourself.

3
I have heard what the talkers were talking, the talk of the
    beginning and the end,
But I do not talk of the beginning or the end.

There was never any more inception than there is now,
Nor any more youth or age than there is now,

And will never be any more perfection than there is now,
Nor any more heaven or hell than there is now.

Urge and urge and urge,
Always the procreant urge of the world.

Out of the dimness opposite equals advance—always substance and
    increase, always sex,
Always a knit of identity—always distinction—always a breed of life.

To elaborate is no avail—learned and unlearned feel that it is so.

Sure as the most certain sure, plumb in the uprights, well entretied,
    braced in the beams,
Stout as a horse, affectionate, haughty, electrical,
I and this mystery here we stand.

Clear and sweet is my soul, and clear and sweet is all that is not my
    soul.

Lack one lacks both, and the unseen is proved by the seen,
Till that becomes unseen and receives proof in its turn.

Showing the best and dividing it from the worst, age vexes age,
Knowing the perfect fitness and equanimity of things, while they
    discuss I am silent, and go bathe and admire myself.

Welcome is every organ and attribute of me, and of any man hearty
    and clean,
Not an inch nor a particle of an inch is vile, and none shall be less
    familiar than the rest.

I am satisfied—I see, dance, laugh, sing,

As God comes a loving bed-fellow and sleeps at my side all night and
    close on the peep of the day,
And leaves for me baskets covered with white towels bulging the house
    with their plenty,
Shall I postpone my acceptation and realization and scream at my eyes,
That they turn from gazing after and down the road,
And forthwith cipher and show me to a cent,
Exactly the contents of one, and exactly the contents of two, and
    which is ahead?

4

Trippers and askers surround me,
People I meet—the effect upon me of my early life, of the ward
    and city I live in, of the nation,
The latest news, discoveries, inventions, societies, authors old and new,
My dinner, dress, associates, looks, business, compliments, dues,
The real or fancied indifference of some man or woman I love,
The sickness of one of my folks, or of myself, or ill-doing, or loss or
    lack of money, or depressions or exaltations,
They come to me days and nights and go from me again,
But they are not the Me myself.

Apart from the pulling and hauling stands what I am,
Stands amused, complacent, compassionating, idle, unitary,
Looks down, is erect, bends an arm on an impalpable certain rest,
Looks with its side-curved head curious what will come next,
Both in and out of the game, and watching and wondering at it.

Backward I see in my own days where I sweated through fog with
    linguists and contenders,
I have no mockings or arguments—I witness and wait.

5

I believe in you my soul—the other I am must not abase itself to
    you,
And you must not be abased to the other.

Loafe with me on the grass—loose the stop from your throat,
Not words, not music or rhyme I want—not custom or lecture,
    not even the best,
Only the lull I like, the hum of your valved voice.

I mind how once we lay such a transparent summer morning,
How you settled your head athwart my hips and gently turned over
    upon me,
And parted the shirt from my bosom-bone, and plunged your tongue
    to my bare-stript heart,
And reached till you felt my beard, and reached till you held my feet.

Swiftly arose and spread around me the peace and knowledge that pass
    all the argument of the earth,
And I know that the hand of God is the elderhand of my own,
And I know that the spirit of God is the brother of my own,
And that all the men ever born are also my brothers, and the women
    my sisters and lovers,
And that a kelson of the creation is love,
And limitless are leaves stiff or drooping in the fields,
And brown ants in the little wells beneath them,
And mossy scabs of the worm fence, and heaped stones, and elder and
    mullen and poke-weed.

6

A child said, What is the grass? fetching it to me with full hands,
How could I answer the child? I do not know what it is any more
    than he.

I guess it must be the flag of my disposition, out of hopeful green
stuff woven.

Or I guess it is the handkerchief of the Lord,
A scented gift and remembrancer designedly dropped,
Bearing the owner's name someway in the corners, that we may see
and remark, and say Whose?

Or I guess the grass is itself a child, the produced babe of the vegetation.

Or I guess it is a uniform hieroglyphic,
And it means, Sprouting alike in broad zones and narrow zones,
Growing among black folks as among white,
Kanuck, Tuckahoe, Congressman, Cuff, I give them the same, I receive
them the same.

And now it seems to me the beautiful uncut hair of graves.

Tenderly will I use you curling grass,
It may be you transpire from the breasts of young men,
It may be if I had known them I would have loved them,
It may be you are from old people and from women, and from
offspring taken soon out of their mothers' laps,
And here you are the mothers' laps.

This grass is very dark to be from the white heads of old mothers,
Darker than the colorless beards of old men,
Dark to come from under the faint red roofs of mouths.

O I perceive after all so many uttering tongues!
And I perceive they do not come from the roofs of mouths for nothing.

I wish I could translate the hints about the dead young men and
women

And the hints about old men and mothers, and the offspring taken
    soon out of their laps.

What do you think has become of the young and old men?
And what do you think has become of the women and children?

They are alive and well somewhere,
The smallest sprout shows there is really no death,
And if ever there was it led forward life, and does not wait at the
    end to arrest it,
And ceased the moment life appeared.

All goes onward and outward—and nothing collapses,
And to die is different from what any one supposed, and luckier.

7
Has any one supposed it lucky to be born?
I hasten to inform him or her it is just as lucky to die, and I know it.

I pass death with the dying, and birth with the new-washed babe,
    and am not contained between my hat and boots,
And peruse manifold objects, no two alike, and every one good,
The earth good, and the stars good, and their adjuncts all good.

I am not an earth nor an adjunct of an earth,
I am the mate and companion of people, all just as immortal and
    fathomless as myself,
They do not know how immortal, but I know.

Every kind for itself and its own—for me mine male and female,
For me all that have been boys and that love women,
For me the man that is proud and feels how it stings to be slighted,
For me the sweetheart and the old maid—for me mothers and the
    mothers of mothers,

For me lips that have smiled, eyes that have shed tears,
For me children and the begetters of children.

Undrape! you are not guilty to me, nor stale nor discarded,
I see through the broadcloth and gingham whether or no,
And am around, tenacious, acquisitive, tireless, and can never be
    shaken away.

8

The little one sleeps in its cradle,
I lift the gauze and look a long time, and silently brush away flies
    with my hand.

The youngster and the red-faced girl turn aside up the bushy hill,
I peeringly view them from the top.

The suicide sprawls on the bloody floor of the bedroom,
It is so—I witnessed the corpse—there the pistol had fallen.

The blab of the pave, the tires of carts and sluff of boot-soles and
    talk of the promenaders,
The heavy omnibus, the driver with his interrogating thumb, the clank
    of the shod horses on the granite floor,
The snow-sleighs, the clinking and shouted jokes and pelts of snow-balls,
The hurrahs for popular favorites, the fury of roused mobs,
The flap of the curtained litter—the sick man inside, borne to the
    hospital,
The meeting of enemies, the sudden oath, the blows and fall,
The excited crowd—the policeman with his star quickly working his
    passage to the centre of the crowd,
The impassive stones that receive and return so many echoes,
The souls moving along—are they invisible while the least atom of
    the stones is visible?

What groans of over-fed or half-starved who fall on the flags sunstruck
or in fits,
What exclamations of women taken suddenly, who hurry home and
give birth to babes,
What living and buried speech is always vibrating here—what howls
restrained by decorum,
Arrests of criminals, slights, adulterous offers made, acceptances,
rejections with convex lips,
I mind them or the resonance of them—I come again and again.

9

The big doors of the country-barn stand open and ready,
The dried grass of the harvest-time loads the slow-drawn wagon,
The clear light plays on the brown gray and green intertinged,
The armfuls are packed to the sagging mow,
I am there—I help—I came stretched atop of the load,
I felt its soft jolts—one leg reclined on the other,
I jump from the cross-beams, and seize the clover and timothy,
And roll head over heels, and tangle my hair full of wisps.

10

Alone far in the wilds and mountains I hunt,
Wandering amazed at my own lightness and glee,
In the late afternoon choosing a safe spot to pass the night,
Kindling a fire and broiling the fresh-killed game,
Soundly falling asleep on the gathered leaves, my dog and gun by my
side.

The Yankee clipper is under her three sky-sails—she cuts the sparkle
and scud,
My eyes settle the land—I bend at her prow or shout joyously from
the deck.

The boatmen and clam-diggers arose early and stopped for me,

I tucked my trowser-ends in my boots and went and had a good time,
You should have been with us that day round the chowder-kettle.

I saw the marriage of the trapper in the open air in the far-west—
    the bride was a red girl,
Her father and his friends sat near by cross-legged and dumbly smoking—
    they had moccasins to their feet and large thick blankets hanging
    from their shoulders,
On a bank lounged the trapper—he was dressed mostly in skins—his
    luxuriant beard and curls protected his neck,
One hand rested on his rifle—the other hand held firmly the wrist of
    the red girl,
She had long eyelashes—her head was bare—her coarse straight locks
    descended upon her voluptuous limbs and reached to her feet.

The runaway slave came to my house and stopped outside,
I heard his motions crackling the twigs of the woodpile,
Through the swung half-door of the kitchen I saw him limpsey and
    weak,
And went where he sat on a log, and led him in and assured him,
And brought water and filled a tub for his sweated body and bruised
    feet,
And gave him a room that entered from my own, and gave him some
    coarse clean clothes,
And remember perfectly well his revolving eyes and his awkwardness,
And remember putting plasters on the galls of his neck and ankles,
He staid with me a week before he was recuperated and passed north,
I had him sit next me at table—my firelock leaned in the corner.

11
Twenty-eight young men bathe by the shore,
Twenty-eight young men, and all so friendly,
Twenty-eight years of womanly life, and all so lonesome.

She owns the fine house by the rise of the bank,
She hides handsome and richly drest aft the blinds of the window.

Which of the young men does she like the best?
Ah the homeliest of them is beautiful to her.

Where are you off to, lady? for I see you,
You splash in the water there, yet stay stock still in your room.

Dancing and laughing along the beach came the twenty-ninth bather,
The rest did not see her, but she saw them and loved them.

The beards of the young men glistened with wet, it ran from their
     long hair,
Little streams passed all over their bodies.

An unseen hand also passed over their bodies,
It descended tremblingly from their temples and ribs.

The young men float on their backs, their white bellies swell to the
     sun—they do not ask who seizes fast to them,
They do not know who puffs and declines with pendant and bending
     arch,
They do not think whom they souse with spray.

12
The butcher-boy puts off his killing-clothes, or sharpens his knife
     at the stall in the market,
I loiter enjoying his repartee and his shuffle and breakdown.

Blacksmiths with grimed and hairy chests environ the anvil,
Each has his main-sledge—they are all out—there is a great heat in
     the fire.

From the cinder-strewed threshold I follow their movements,
The lithe sheer of their waists plays even with their massive arms,
Overhand the hammers roll—overhand so slow—overhand so sure,
They do not hasten, each man hits in his place.

13

The negro holds firmly the reins of his four horses—the block swags
    underneath on its tied-over chain,
The negro that drives the huge dray of the stone-yard—steady and
    tall he stands poised on one leg on the string-piece,
His blue shirt exposes his ample neck and breast and loosens over his
    hip-band,
His glance is calm and commanding—he tosses the slouch of his hat
    away from his forehead,
The sun falls on his crispy hair and moustache—falls on the black of
    his polished and perfect limbs.

I behold the picturesque giant and love him—and I do not stop there,
I go with the team also.

In me the caresser of life wherever moving—backward as well as
    forward slueing,
To niches aside and junior bending.

Oxen that rattle the yoke or halt in the shade, what is that you express
    in your eyes?
It seems to me more than all the print I have read in my life.

My tread scares the wood-drake and wood-duck on my distant and
    daylong ramble,
They rise together, they slowly circle around.
I believe in those winged purposes,
And acknowledge the red yellow and white playing within me,
And consider the green and violet and the tufted crown intentional,

And do not call the tortoise unworthy because she is not something else,
And the mockingbird in the swamp never studied the gamut, yet trills
    pretty well to me,
And the look of the bay mare shames silliness out of me.

14

The wild gander leads his flock through the cool night,
Ya-honk! he says, and sounds it down to me like an invitation,
The pert may suppose it meaningless, but I listen closer,
I find its purpose and place up there toward the November sky.

The sharp-hoofed moose of the north, the cat on the house-sill, the
    chickadee, the prairie-dog,
The litter of the grunting sow as they tug at her teats,
The brood of the turkey-hen, and she with her half-spread wings,
I see in them and myself the same old law.

The press of my foot to the earth springs a hundred affections,
They scorn the best I can do to relate them.

I am enamoured of growing outdoors,
Of men that live among cattle or taste of the ocean or woods,
Of the builders and steerers of ships, of the wielders of axes and mauls,
    of the drivers of horses,
I can eat and sleep with them week in and week out.

What is commonest and cheapest and nearest and easiest is Me,
Me going in for my chances, spending for vast returns,
Adorning myself to bestow myself on the first that will take me,
Not asking the sky to come down to my good will,
Scattering it freely forever.

15

The pure contralto sings in the organ loft,

The carpenter dresses his plank — the tongue of his foreplane
   whistles its wild ascending lisp,
The married and unmarried children ride home to their thanksgiving
   dinner,
The pilot seizes the king-pin, he heaves down with a strong arm,
The mate stands braced in the whale-boat, lance and harpoon are ready,
The duck-shooter walks by silent and cautious stretches,
The deacons are ordained with crossed hands at the altar,
The spinning-girl retreats and advances to the hum of the big wheel,
The farmer stops by the bars of a Sunday and looks at the oats and rye,
The lunatic is carried at last to the asylum a confirmed case,
He will never sleep any more as he did in the cot in his mother's
   bedroom,
The jour printer with gray head and gaunt jaws works at his case,
He turns his quid of tobacco, his eyes get blurred with the manuscript,
The malformed limbs are tied to the anatomist's table,
What is removed drops horribly in a pail,
The quadroon girl is sold at the stand — the drunkard nods by the
   bar-room stove,
The machinist rolls up his sleeves — the policeman travels his beat —
   the gate-keeper marks who pass,
The young fellow drives the express-wagon — I love him though I do
   not know him,
The half-breed straps on his light boots to compete in the race,
The western turkey-shooting draws old and young — some lean on their
   rifles, some sit on logs,
Out from the crowd steps the marksman and takes his position and
   levels his piece,
The groups of newly-come immigrants cover the wharf or levee,
The woolly-pates hoe in the sugar-field, the overseer views them from
   his saddle,
The bugle calls in the ball-room, the gentlemen run for their partners,
   the dancers bow to each other,

The youth lies awake in the cedar-roofed garret and harks to the
  musical rain,

The Wolverine sets traps on the creek that helps fill the Huron,

The reformer ascends the platform, he spouts with his mouth and nose,

The squaw wrapt in her yellow-hemmed cloth is offering moccasins
  and bead-bags for sale,

The connoisseur peers along the exhibition-gallery with half-shut eyes
  bent sideways,

The deck-hands make fast the steamboat, the plank is thrown for the
  shore-going passengers,

The young sister holds out the skein, the elder sister winds it off in a
  ball and stops now and then for the knots,

The one-year wife is recovering and happy, a week ago she bore her
  first child,

The clean-haired Yankee girl works with her sewing-machine or in the
  factory or mill,

The nine months' gone is in the parturition chamber, her faintness and
  pains are advancing,

The paving-man leans on his two-handed rammer—the reporter's lead
  flies swiftly over the note-book—the sign-painter is lettering with
  red and gold,

The canal boy trots on the tow-path—the book-keeper counts at his
  desk—the shoemaker waxes his thread,

The conductor beats time for the band and all the performers follow him,

The child is baptised—the convert is making the first professions,

The regatta is spread on the bay—how the white sails sparkle!

The drover watches his drove, he sings out to them that would stray,

The pedlar sweats with his pack on his back—the purchaser higgles
  about the odd cent,

The camera and plate are prepared, the lady must sit for her
  daguerreotype,

The bride unrumples her white dress, the minute-hand of the clock
  moves slowly,

The opium eater reclines with rigid head and just-opened lips,
The prostitute draggles her shawl, her bonnet bobs on her tipsy and
pimpled neck,
The crowd laugh at her blackguard oaths, the men jeer and wink to
each other,
(Miserable! I do not laugh at your oaths nor jeer you,)
The President holds a cabinet council, he is surrounded by the great
secretaries,
On the piazza walk five friendly matrons with twined arms,
The crew of the fish-smack pack repeated layers of halibut in the hold,
The Missourian crosses the plains toting his wares and his cattle,
The fare-collector goes through the train—he gives notice by the
jingling of loose change,
The floor-men are laying the floor—the tinners are tinning the roof—
the masons are calling for mortar,
In single file each shouldering his hod pass onward the laborers,
Seasons pursuing each other the indescribable crowd is gathered—it is
the Fourth of July—what salutes of cannon and small arms!

Seasons pursuing each other the plougher ploughs and the mower
mows and the winter-grain falls in the ground,
Off on the lakes the pike-fisher watches and waits by the hole in the
frozen surface,
The stumps stand thick round the clearing, the squatter strikes deep
with his axe,
The flatboatmen make fast toward dusk near the cotton-wood or
pecan-trees,
The coon-seekers go now through the regions of the Red river, or
through those drained by the Tennessee, or through those of
the Arkansas,
The torches shine in the dark that hangs on the Chattahoochee or
Altamahaw,
Patriarchs sit at supper with sons and grandsons and great grandsons
around them,

In walls of adobie, in canvas tents, rest hunters and trappers after
  their day's sport.

The city sleeps and the country sleeps,
The living sleep for their time, the dead sleep for their time,
The old husband sleeps by his wife and the young husband sleeps by
  his wife,
And these one and all tend inward to me, and I tend outward to them,
And such as it is to be of these more or less I am.

16

I am of old and young, of the foolish as much as the wise,
Regardless of others, ever regardful of others,
Maternal as well as paternal, a child as well as a man,
Stuffed with the stuff that is coarse, and stuffed with the stuff that is
  fine,
One of the great nations, the nation of many nations — the smallest the
  same and the largest the same,
A southerner soon as a northerner, a planter nonchalant and hospitable,
A Yankee bound my own way, ready for trade, my joints the limberest
  joints on earth and the sternest joints on earth,
A Kentuckian walking the vale of the Elkhorn in my deer-skin leggings,
A boatman over the lakes or bays or along coasts — a Hoosier, a Badger,
  a Buckeye,
A Louisianian or Georgian, a poke-easy from sandhills and pines,
At home on Canadian snow-shoes or up in the bush, or with fishermen
  off Newfoundland,
At home in the fleet of ice-boats, sailing with the rest and tacking,
At home on the hills of Vermont or in the woods of Maine or the
  Texan ranch,
Comrade of Californians — comrade of free northwesterners, loving
  their big proportions,
Comrade of raftsmen and coalmen — comrade of all who shake hands
  and welcome to drink and meat,

A learner with the simplest, a teacher of the thoughtfulest,
A novice beginning experient of myriads of seasons,
Of every hue and trade and rank, of every caste and religion,
Not merely of the New World but of Africa Europe or Asia—a
    wandering savage,
A farmer, mechanic, or artist, a gentleman, sailor, lover or quaker,
A prisoner, fancy-man, rowdy, lawyer, physician or priest.

I resist anything better than my own diversity,
And breathe the air and leave plenty after me,
And am not stuck up, and am in my place.

The moth and the fish-eggs are in their place,
The suns I see and the suns I cannot see are in their place,
The palpable is in its place and the impalpable is in its place.

17
These are the thoughts of all men in all ages and lands, they are
    not original with me,
If they are not yours as much as mine they are nothing or next to
    nothing,
If they are not the riddle and the untying of the riddle they are
    nothing,
If they are not just as close as they are distant they are nothing.

This is the grass that grows wherever the land is and the water is,
This is the common air that bathes the globe.

This is the breath of laws and songs and behaviour,
This is the tasteless water of souls—this is the true sustenance,
It is for the illiterate, it is for the judges of the supreme court, it is for
    the federal capitol and the state capitols,
It is for the admirable communes of literary men and composers and
    singers and lecturers and engineers and savans,
It is for the endless races of working people and farmers and seamen.

18

This is the trill of a thousand clear cornets and scream of the octave
    flute and strike of triangles.

I play not a march for victors only—I play great marches for conquered
    and slain persons.

Have you heard that it was good to gain the day?
I also say it is good to fall—battles are lost in the same spirit in which
    they are won.

I sound triumphal drums for the dead, I fling through my embouchures
    the loudest and gayest music to them,
Vivas to those who have failed, and to those whose war-vessels sank in
    the sea, and those themselves who sank in the sea,
And to all generals that lost engagements, and all overcome heroes,
    and the numberless unknown heroes equal to the greatest heroes
    known.

19

This is the meal pleasantly set—this is the meat and drink for natural
    hunger,
It is for the wicked just the same as the righteous—I make
    appointments with all,
I will not have a single person slighted or left away,
The kept-woman and sponger and thief are hereby invited, the
    heavy-lipped slave is invited—the venerealee is invited,
There shall be no difference between them and the rest.

This is the press of a bashful hand—this is the float and odor of hair,
This is the touch of my lips to yours—this is the murmur of yearning,
This is the far-off depth and height reflecting my own face,
This is the thoughtful merge of myself and the outlet again.

Do you guess I have some intricate purpose?
Well I have—for the April rain has, and the mica on the side of a rock
    has.

Do you take it I would astonish?
Does the daylight astonish? or the early redstart twittering through
    the woods?
Do I astonish more than they?

This hour I tell things in confidence,
I might not tell everybody but I will tell you.

20
Who goes there! hankering, gross, mystical, nude?
How is it I extract strength from the beef I eat?

What is a man anyhow? what am I? and what are you?
All I mark as my own you shall offset it with your own,
Else it were time lost listening to me.

I do not snivel that snivel the world over,
That months are vacuums and the ground but wallow and filth,
That life is a suck and a sell, and nothing remains at the end but
    threadbare crape and tears.

Whimpering and truckling fold with powders for invalids—conformity
    goes to the fourth-removed,
I cock my hat as I please indoors or out.

Shall I pray? shall I venerate and be ceremonious?
I have pried through the strata and analyzed to a hair,
And counselled with doctors and calculated close and found no sweeter
    fat than sticks to my own bones.

In all people I see myself, none more and not one a barley-corn less,
And the good or bad I say of myself I say of them.

And I know I am solid and sound,
To me the converging objects of the universe perpetually flow,
All are written to me, and I must get what the writing means.

And I know I am deathless,
I know this orbit of mine cannot be swept by a carpenter's compass,
I know I shall not pass like a child's carlacue cut with a burnt stick
    at night.

I know I am august,
I do not trouble my spirit to vindicate itself or be understood,
I see that the elementary laws never apologize,
I reckon I behave no prouder than the level I plant my house by after all.

I exist as I am, that is enough,
If no other in the world be aware I sit content,
And if each and all be aware I sit content.

One world is aware, and by far the largest to me, and that is myself,
And whether I come to my own today or in ten thousand or ten
    million years,
I can cheerfully take it now, or with equal cheerfulness I can wait.

My foothold is tenoned and mortised in granite,
I laugh at what you call dissolution,
And I know the amplitude of time.

21
I am the poet of the body,
And I am the poet of the soul.

The pleasures of heaven are with me, and the pains of hell are with me,
The first I graft and increase upon myself—the latter I translate into a
new tongue.

I am the poet of the woman the same as the man,
And I say it is as great to be a woman as to be a man,
And I say there is nothing greater than the mother of men.

I chant a new chant of dilation or pride,

We have had ducking and deprecating about enough,
I show that size is only development.

Have you outstript the rest? are you the President?
It is a trifle—they will more than arrive there every one, and still
pass on.

I am he that walks with the tender and growing night,
I call to the earth and sea half-held by the night.

Press close bare-bosomed night! Press close magnetic nourishing night!
Night of south winds! Night of the large few stars!
Still nodding night! Mad naked summer night!

Smile O voluptuous cool-breathed earth!
Earth of the slumbering and liquid trees!
Earth of departed sunset! Earth of the mountains misty-topt!
Earth of the vitreous pour of the full moon just tinged with blue!
Earth of shine and dark mottling the tide of the river!
Earth of the limpid gray of clouds brighter and clearer for my sake!
Far-swooping elbowed earth! Rich apple-blossomed earth!
Smile, for your lover comes!

Prodigal! you have given me love! Therefore I to you give love!
O unspeakable passionate love!

Thruster holding me tight and that I hold tight!
We hurt each other as the bridegroom and the bride hurt each other.

22
You sea! I resign myself to you also—I guess what you mean,
I behold from the beach your crooked inviting fingers,
I believe you refuse to go back without feeling of me,
We must have a turn together—I undress—hurry me out of sight of
    the land,
Cushion me soft, rock me in billowy drowse,
Dash me with amorous wet—I can repay you.

Sea of stretched ground-swells!
Sea breathing broad and convulsive breaths!
Sea of the brine of life! sea of unshovelled and always-ready graves!
Howler and scooper of storms! capricious and dainty sea!
I am integral with you—I too am of one phase and of all phases.

Partaker of influx and efflux—extoller of hate and conciliation,
Extoller of amies and those that sleep in each others' arms.

I am he attesting sympathy;
Shall I make my list of things in the house and skip the house that
    supports them?

I am the poet of commonsense and of the demonstrable and of
    immortality,
And am not the poet of goodness only—I do not decline to be the
    poet of wickedness also.

Washes and razors for foofoos—for me freckles and a bristling beard.

What blurt is it about virtue and about vice?
Evil propels me, and reform of evil propels me—I stand indifferent,

My gait is no fault-finder's or rejecter's gait,
I moisten the roots of all that has grown.

Did you fear some scrofula out of the unflagging pregnancy?
Did you guess the celestial laws are yet to be worked over and rectified?

I step up to say that what we do is right and what we affirm is right—
    and some is only the ore of right,
Witnesses of us—one side a balance and the antipodal side a balance,
Soft doctrine as steady help as stable doctrine,
Thoughts and deeds of the present our rouse and early start.

This minute that comes to me over the past decillions,
There is no better than it and now.

What behaved well in the past or behaves well today is not such a
    wonder,
The wonder is always and always how there can be a mean man or an
    infidel.

23
Endless unfolding of words of ages!
And mine a word of the modern—a word en masse.

A word of the faith that never balks,
One time as good as another time—here or henceforward it is all the
    same to me.

A word of reality—materialism first and last imbuing.

Hurrah for positive science! Long live exact demonstration!
Fetch stonecrop and mix it with cedar and branches of lilac,
This is the lexicographer or chemist—this made a grammar of the old
    cartouches,

These mariners put the ship through dangerous unknown seas,
This is the geologist—and this works with the scalpel—and this is a
mathematician.

Gentlemen I receive you, and attach and clasp hands with you,
The facts are useful and real—they are not my dwelling—I enter by
them to an area of the dwelling.

I am less the reminder of property or qualities, and more the reminder
of life,
And go on the square for my own sake and for other's sake,
And make short account of neuters and geldings, and favor men and
women fully equipped,
And beat the gong of revolt, and stop with fugitives and them that plot
and conspire.

24

Walt Whitman, an American, one of the roughs, a kosmos,
Disorderly fleshy and sensual, eating drinking and breeding,
No sentimentalist—no stander above men and women or apart from
them—no more modest than immodest.

Unscrew the locks from the doors!
Unscrew the doors themselves from their jambs!

Whoever degrades another degrades me, and whatever is done or said
returns at last to me,
And whatever I do or say I also return.

Through me the afflatus surging and surging—through me the current
and index.

I speak the pass-word primeval—I give the sign of democracy,
By God! I will accept nothing which all cannot have their counterpart
of on the same terms.

Through me many long dumb voices,
Voices of the interminable generations of slaves,
Voices of prostitutes and of deformed persons,
Voices of the diseased and despairing, and of thieves and dwarfs,
Voices of cycles of preparation and accretion,
And of the threads that connect the stars—and of wombs, and of the
    father-stuff,
And of the rights of them the others are down upon,
Of the trivial and flat and foolish and despised,
Of fog in the air and beetles rolling balls of dung.

Through me forbidden voices,
Voices of sexes and lusts—voices veiled, and I remove the veil,
Voices indecent by me clarified and transfigured.

I do not press my finger across my mouth,
I keep as delicate around the bowels as around the head and heart,
Copulation is no more rank to me than death is.

I believe in the flesh and the appetites,
Seeing hearing and feeling are miracles, and each part and tag of me
    is a miracle.

Divine am I inside and out, and I make holy whatever I touch or am
    touched from,
The scent of these arm-pits is aroma finer than prayer,
This head is more than churches or bibles or creeds.

If I worship one thing more than another it shall be the spread of my
    own body, or any part of it.
Translucent mould of me it shall be you,
Shaded ledges and rests, firm masculine coulter, it shall be you,
Whatever goes to the tilth of me it shall be you,
You my rich blood, your milky stream pale strippings of my life,

Breast that presses against other breasts it shall be you,
My brain it shall be your occult convolutions,
Root of washed sweet-flag, timorous pond-snipe, nest of guarded
    duplicate eggs, it shall be you,
Mixed tussled hay of head and beard and brawn it shall be you,
Trickling sap of maple, fibre of manly wheat, it shall be you,
Sun so generous it shall be you,
Vapors lighting and shading my face it shall be you,
You sweaty brooks and dews it shall be you,
Winds whose soft-tickling genitals rub against me it shall be you,
Broad muscular fields, branches of live oak, loving lounger in my
    winding paths, it shall be you,
Hands I have taken, face I have kissed, mortal I have ever touched,
    it shall be you.

I dote on myself—there is that lot of me, and all so luscious,
Each moment and whatever happens thrills me with joy.

I cannot tell how my ankles bend, nor whence the cause of my
    faintest wish,
Nor the cause of the friendship I emit, nor the cause of the friendship
    I take again.

To walk up my stoop is unaccountable, I pause to consider if it
    really be,
That I eat and drink is spectacle enough for the great authors and
    schools,
A morning-glory at my window satisfies me more than the
    metaphysics of books.

To behold the daybreak!
The little light fades the immense and diaphanous shadows,
The air tastes good to my palate.

Hefts of the moving world at innocent gambols, silently rising,
    freshly exuding,
Scooting obliquely high and low.

Something I cannot see puts upward libidinous prongs,
Seas of bright juice suffuse heaven.

The earth by the sky staid with—the daily close of their junction,
The heaved challenge from the east that moment over my head,
The mocking taunt, See then whether you shall be master!

25

Dazzling and tremendous how quick the sunrise would kill me,
If I could not now and always send sunrise out of me.

We also ascend dazzling and tremendous as the sun,
We found our own my soul in the calm and cool of the daybreak.

My voice goes after what my eyes cannot reach,
With the twirl of my tongue I encompass worlds and volumes of
    worlds.

Speech is the twin of my vision—it is unequal to measure itself.

It provokes me forever,
It says sarcastically, Walt, you understand enough—why don't you
    let it out then?

Come now I will not be tantalized—you conceive too much of
    articulation.

Do you not know how the buds beneath are folded?
Waiting in gloom protected by frost,
The dirt receding before my prophetical screams,

I underlying causes to balance them at last,
My knowledge my live parts—it keeping tally with the meaning of
    things,
Happiness—which whoever hears me let him or her set out in
    search of this day.

My final merit I refuse you—I refuse putting from me the best I am.

Encompass worlds but never try to encompass me,
I crowd your noisiest talk by looking toward you.

Writing and talk do not prove me,
I carry the plenum of proof and every thing else in my face,
With the hush of my lips I confound the topmost skeptic.

26
I think I will do nothing for a long time but listen,
And accrue what I hear into myself—and let sounds contribute
    toward me.

I hear the bravuras of birds, the bustle of growing wheat, gossip
    of flames, clack of sticks cooking my meals.

I hear the sound of the human voice—a sound I love,
I hear all sounds as they are tuned to their uses, sounds of the city
    and sounds out of the city—sounds of the day and night,
Talkative young ones to those that like them—the recitative of
    fish-pedlars and fruit-pedlars—the loud laugh of work-people
    at their meals,
The angry bass of disjointed friendship—the faint tones of the sick,
The judge with hands tight to the desk, his shaky lips pronouncing
    a death-sentence,
The heave'e'yo of stevedores unlading ships by the wharves—the
    refrain of the anchor-lifters,

The ring of alarm-bells—the cry of fire—the whirr of swift-streaking
    engines and hose-carts with premonitory tinkles and colored lights,
The steam-whistle—the solid roll of the train of approaching cars,
The slow-march played at night at the head of the association,
They go to guard some corpse—the flag-tops are draped with black
    muslin.

I hear the violincello or man's heart complaint,
And hear the keyed cornet or else the echo of sunset.

I hear the chorus—it is a grand-opera, this indeed is music!

A tenor large and fresh as the creation fills me,
The orbic flex of his mouth is pouring and filling me full.

I hear the trained soprano—she convulses me like the climax of my
    love-grip,
The orchestra whirls me wider than Uranus flies,
It wrenches unnamable ardors from my breast,
It throbs me to gulps of the farthest down horror,
It sails me, I dab with bare feet, they are licked by the indolent waves,
I am exposed, cut by bitter and poisoned hail,
Steeped amid honeyed morphine, my windpipe squeezed in the fakes
    of death,
Let up again to feel the puzzle of puzzles,
And that we call Being.

27
To be in any form, what is that?
If nothing lay more developed the quahaug and its callous shell were
    enough.

Mine is no callous shell,
I have instant conductors all over me whether I pass or stop,
They seize every object and lead it harmlessly through me.

I merely stir, press, feel with my fingers, and am happy,
To touch my person to some one else's is about as much as I can
stand.

28
Is this then a touch? quivering me to a new identity,
Flames and ether making a rush for my veins,
Treacherous tip of me reaching and crowding to help them,
My flesh and blood playing out lightning, to strike what is hardly
different from myself,
On all sides prurient provokers stiffening my limbs,
Straining the udder of my heart for its withheld drip,
Behaving licentious toward me, taking no denial,
Depriving me of my best as for a purpose,
Unbuttoning my clothes and holding me by the bare waist,
Deluding my confusion with the calm of the sunlight and pasture
fields,
Immodestly sliding the fellow-senses away,
They bribed to swap off with touch, and go and graze at the edges
of me,
No consideration, no regard for my draining strength or my anger,
Fetching the rest of the herd around to enjoy them awhile,
Then all uniting to stand on a headland and worry me.

The sentries desert every other part of me,
They have left me helpless to a red marauder,
They all come to the headland to witness and assist against me.

I am given up by traitors,
I talk wildly—I have lost my wits—I and nobody else am the
greatest traitor,
I went myself first to the headland—my own hands carried me there.

You villain touch! what are you doing? my breath is tight in its
    throat,
Unclench your floodgates! you are too much for me.

29
Blind loving wrestling touch! sheathed hooded sharp-toothed touch!
Did it make you ache so leaving me?

Parting tracked by arriving—perpetual payment of the perpetual loan,
Rich showering rain, and recompense richer afterward.

Sprouts take and accumulate—stand by the curb prolific and vital,
Landscapes projected masculine full-sized and golden.

30
All truths wait in all things,
They neither hasten their own delivery nor resist it,
They do not need the obstetric forceps of the surgeon,
The insignificant is as big to me as any,
What is less or more than a touch?

Logic and sermons never convince,
The damp of the night drives deeper into my soul.

Only what proves itself to every man and woman is so,
Only what nobody denies is so.

A minute and a drop of me settle my brain,
I believe the soggy clods shall become lovers and lamps,
And a compend of compends is the meat of a man or woman,
And a summit and flower there is the feeling they have for each other,
And they are to branch boundlessly out of that lesson until it becomes
    omnific,
And until every one shall delight us, and we them.

31

I believe a leaf of grass is no less than the journeywork of the stars,
And the pismire is equally perfect, and a grain of sand, and the egg
     of the wren,
And the tree-toad is a chef-d'œuvre for the highest,
And the running blackberry would adorn the parlors of heaven,
And the narrowest hinge in my hand puts to scorn all machinery,
And the cow crunching with depressed head surpasses any statue,
And a mouse is miracle enough to stagger sextillions of infidels,
And I could come every afternoon of my life to look at the farmer's
     girl boiling her iron tea-kettle and baking shortcake.

I find I incorporate gneiss and coal and long-threaded moss and
     fruits and grains and esculent roots,
And am stucco'd with quadrupeds and birds all over,
And have distanced what is behind me for good reasons,
And call any thing close again when I desire it.

In vain the speeding or shyness,
In vain the plutonic rocks send their old heat against my approach,
In vain the mastodon retreats beneath its own powdered bones,
In vain objects stand leagues off and assume manifold shapes,
In vain the ocean settling in hollows and the great monsters lying low,
In vain the buzzard houses herself with the sky,
In vain the snake slides through the creepers and logs,
In vain the elk takes to the inner passes of the woods,
In vain the razor-billed auk sails far north to Labrador,
I follow quickly, I ascend to the nest in the fissure of the cliff.

32

I think I could turn and live awhile with the animals, they are so
     placid and self-contained,
I stand and look at them sometimes half the day long.

They do not sweat and whine about their condition,
They do not lie awake in the dark and weep for their sins,
They do not make me sick discussing their duty to God,
Not one is dissatisfied—not one is demented with the mania of
    owning things,
Not one kneels to another nor to his kind that lived thousands of
    years ago,
Not one is respectable or unhappy over the whole earth.

So they show their relations to me and I accept them,
They bring me tokens of myself—they evince them plainly in their
    possession.

I do not know where they got those tokens,
I must have passed that way untold times ago and negligently dropt
    them,
Myself moving forward then and now and forever,
Gathering and showing more always and with velocity,
Infinite and omnigenous and the like of these among them,
Not too exclusive toward the reachers of my remembrancers,
Picking out here one that shall be my amie,
Choosing to go with him on brotherly terms.

A gigantic beauty of a stallion, fresh and responsive to my caresses,
Head high in the forehead and wide between the ears,
Limbs glossy and supple, tail dusting the ground,
Eyes well apart and full of sparkling wickedness—ears finely cut and
    flexibly moving.

His nostrils dilate, my heels embrace him, his well-built limbs
    tremble with pleasure, we speed around and return.

I but use you a moment and then I resign you stallion, and do not
    need your paces, and outgallop them,
And myself as I stand or sit pass faster than you.

33

Swift wind! Space! My soul! now I know it is true what I guessed
    at,
What I guessed when I loafed on the grass,
What I guessed while I lay alone in my bed, and again as I walked
    the beach under the paling stars of the morning.

My ties and ballasts leave me—I travel—I sail—my elbows rest in the
    sea-gaps,
I skirt the sierras—my palms cover continents,
I am afoot with my vision.

By the city's quadrangular houses—in log-huts—or camping with
    lumbermen,
Along the ruts of the turnpike—along the dry gulch and rivulet bed,
Hoeing my onion-patch, and rows of carrots and parsnips—crossing
    savannas—trailing in forests,
Prospecting—gold-digging—girdling the trees of a new purchase,
Scorched ankle-deep by the hot sand—hauling my boat down the
    shallow river,
Where the panther walks to and fro on a limb overhead—where the
    buck turns furiously at the hunter,
Where the rattlesnake suns his flabby length on a rock—where the
    otter is feeding on fish,
Where the alligator in his tough pimples sleeps by the bayou,
Where the black bear is searching for roots or honey—where the
    beaver pats the mud with his paddle-tail,
Over the growing sugar—over the cotton plant—over the rice in its
    low moist field,
Over the sharp-peaked farmhouse with its scalloped scum and slender
    shoots from the gutters,
Over the western persimmon—over the long-leaved corn and the
    delicate blue-flowered flax,

Over the white and brown buckwheat, a hummer and a buzzer there
    with the rest,

Over the dusky green of the rye as it ripples and shades in the breeze,

Scaling mountains, pulling myself cautiously up, holding on by low
    scragged limbs,

Walking the path worn in the grass and beat through the leaves of
    the brush,

Where the quail is whistling betwixt the woods and the wheat-lot,

Where the bat flies in the July eve—where the great gold-bug drops
    through the dark,

Where the flails keep time on the barn floor,

Where the brook puts out of the roots of the old tree and flows to
    the meadow,

Where cattle stand and shake away flies with the tremulous shuddering
    of their hides,

Where the cheese-cloth hangs in the kitchen, and andirons straddle the
    hearth-slab, and cobwebs fall in festoons from the rafters,

Where trip-hammers crash—where the press is whirling its cylinders,

Wherever the human heart beats with terrible throes out of its ribs,

Where the pear-shaped balloon is floating aloft, floating in it myself
    and looking composedly down,

Where the life-car is drawn on the slip-noose—where the heat hatches
    pale-green eggs in the dented sand,

Where the she-whale swims with her calves and never forsakes them,

Where the steam-ship trails hindways its long pennant of smoke,

Where the ground-shark's fin cuts like a black chip out of the water,

Where the half-burned brig is riding on unknown currents,

Where shells grow to her slimy deck, and the dead are corrupting below,

Where the striped and starred flag is borne at the head of the regiments,

Approaching Manhattan, up by the long-stretching island,

Under Niagara, the cataract falling like a veil over my countenance,

Upon a door-step—upon the horse-block of hard wood outside,

Upon the race-course, or enjoying picnics or jigs or a good game of
    base-ball,

At he-festivals with blackguard jibes and ironical license and bull-dances
and drinking and laughter,

At the cider-mill, tasting the sweet of the brown sqush, sucking the
juice through a straw,

At apple-peelings, wanting kisses for all the red fruit I find,

At musters and beach-parties and friendly bees and huskings and
house-raisings,

Where the mockingbird sounds his delicious gurgles, and cackles and
screams and weeps,

Where the hay-rick stands in the barn-yard, and the dry-stalks are
scattered, and the brood cow waits in the hovel,

Where the bull advances to do his masculine work, and the stud to
the mare, and the cock is treading the hen,

Where the heifers browse, and the geese nip their food with short jerks,

Where the sun-down shadows lengthen over the limitless and
lonesome prairie,

Where the herds of buffalo make a crawling spread of the square miles
far and near,

Where the humming-bird shimmers—where the neck of the long-lived
swan is curving and winding,

Where the laughing-gull scoots by the slappy shore and laughs her
near-human laugh,

Where bee-hives range on a gray bench in the garden half-hid by the
high weeds,

Where the band-necked partridges roost in a ring on the ground
with their heads out,

Where burial coaches enter the arched gates of a cemetery,

Where winter wolves bark amid wastes of snow and icicled trees,

Where the yellow-crowned heron comes to the edge of the marsh at
night and feeds upon small crabs,

Where the splash of swimmers and divers cools the warm noon,

Where the katy-did works her chromatic reed on the walnut-tree
over the well,

Through patches of citrons and cucumbers with silver-wired leaves,

Through the salt-lick or orange glade, or under conical firs,
Through the gymnasium—through the curtained saloon—through
the office or public hall,
Pleased with the native and pleased with the foreign—pleased with
the new and old,
Pleased with women, the homely as well as the handsome,
Pleased with the quakeress as she puts off her bonnet and talks
melodiously,
Pleased with the primitive tunes of the choir of the whitewashed church,
Pleased with the earnest words of the sweating Methodist preacher,
or any preacher—impressed seriously at the camp-meeting,
Looking in at the shop-windows in Broadway the whole forenoon—
pressing the flesh of my nose to the thick plate-glass,
Wandering the same afternoon with my face turned up to the clouds,
My right and left arms round the sides of two friends and I in the
middle,
Coming home with the bearded and dark-cheeked bush-boy, riding
behind him at the drape of the day,
Far from the settlements studying the print of animals' feet, or the
moccasin print,
By the cot in the hospital reaching lemonade to a feverish patient,
By the coffined corpse when all is still, examining with a candle,
Voyaging to every port to dicker and adventure,
Hurrying with the modern crowd, as eager and fickle as any,
Hot toward one I hate, ready in my madness to knife him,
Solitary at midnight in my back yard, my thoughts gone from me
a long while,
Walking the old hills of Judea with the beautiful gentle god by my
side,
Speeding through space—speeding through heaven and the stars,
Speeding amid the seven satellites and the broad ring and the diameter
of eighty thousand miles,
Speeding with tailed meteors—throwing fire-balls like the rest,
Carrying the crescent child that carries its own full mother in its belly:

Storming enjoying planning loving cautioning,
Backing and filling, appearing and disappearing,
I tread day and night such roads.

I visit the orchards of God and look at the spheric product,
And look at quintillions ripened, and look at quintillions green.

I fly the flight of the fluid and swallowing soul,
My course runs below the soundings of plummets.

I help myself to material and immaterial,
No guard can shut me off, no law can prevent me.

I anchor my ship for a little while only,
My messengers continually cruise away or bring their returns to me.

I go hunting polar furs and the seal—leaping chasms with a
    pike-pointed staff—clinging to topples of brittle and blue.

I ascend to the foretruck, I take my place late at night in the crow's
    nest, we sail through the arctic sea—it is plenty light enough,
Through the clear atmosphere I stretch around on the wonderful beauty,
The enormous masses of ice pass me and I pass them—the scenery is
    plain in all directions,
The white-topped mountains point up in the distance—I fling out my
    fancies toward them,
We are about approaching some great battlefield in which we are soon
    to be engaged,
We pass the colossal outposts of the encampment—we pass with still
    feet and caution,
Or we are entering by the suburbs some vast and ruined city, the blocks
    and fallen architecture more than all the living cities of the globe.

I am a free companion—I bivouac by invading watchfires.

I turn the bridegroom out of bed and stay with the bride myself,
And tighten her all night to my thighs and lips.

My voice is the wife's voice, the screech by the rail of the stairs,
They fetch my man's body up dripping and drowned.

I understand the large hearts of heroes,
The courage of present times and all times,
How the skipper saw the crowded and rudderless wreck of the
     steam-ship, and death chasing it up and down the storm,
How he knuckled tight and gave not back one inch, and was faithful
     of days and faithful of nights,
And chalked in large letters on a board, Be of good cheer, We will
     not desert you,
How he saved the drifting company at last,
How the lank loose-gowned women looked when boated from the
     side of their prepared graves,
How the silent old-faced infants, and the lifted sick, and the
     sharp-lipped unshaved men,
All this I swallow and it tastes good—I like it well, and it becomes
     mine,
I am the man—I suffered—I was there.

The disdain and calmness of martyrs,
The mother condemned for a witch and burnt with dry wood,
     and her children gazing on,
The hounded slave that flags in the race and leans by the fence,
     blowing and covered with sweat,
The twinges that sting like needles his legs and neck,
The murderous buckshot and the bullets,
All these I feel or am.

I am the hounded slave, I wince at the bite of the dogs,
Hell and despair are upon me, crack and again crack the marksmen,

I clutch the rails of the fence, my gore dribs thinned with the ooze
 of my skin,
I fall on the weeds and stones,
The riders spur their unwilling horses and haul close,
They taunt my dizzy ears, they beat me violently over the head with
 their whip-stocks.

Agonies are one of my changes of garments,
I do not ask the wounded person how he feels—I myself become the
 wounded person,
My hurt turns livid upon me as I lean on a cane and observe.

I am the mashed fireman with breastbone broken—tumbling walls
 buried me in their debris,
Heat and smoke I inspired—I heard the yelling shouts of my comrades,
I heard the distant click of their picks and shovels,
They have cleared the beams away—they tenderly lift me forth.

I lie in the night air in my red shirt—the pervading hush is for my sake,
Painless after all I lie, exhausted but not so unhappy,
White and beautiful are the faces around me—the heads are bared of
 their fire-caps,
The kneeling crowd fades with the light of the torches.

Distant and dead resuscitate,
They show as the dial or move as the hands of me—and I am the
 clock myself.

I am an old artillerist, and tell of some fort's bombardment, and am
 there again.

Again the reveille of drummers, again the attacking cannon and mortars
 and howitzers,
Again the attacked send their cannon responsive.

I take part—I see and hear the whole,
The cries and curses and roar—the plaudits for well-aimed shots,
The ambulanza slowly passing and trailing its red drip,
Workmen searching after damages and to make indispensable repairs,
The fall of grenades through the rent roof—the fan-shaped explosion,
The whizz of limbs heads stone wood and iron high in the air.

Again gurgles the mouth of my dying general—he furiously waves
    with his hand,
He gasps through the clot, Mind not me—mind—the entrenchments.

34

I tell not the fall of Alamo, not one escaped to tell the fall of Alamo,
The hundred and fifty are dumb yet at Alamo.

Hear now the tale of a jetblack sunrise,
Hear of the murder in cold blood of four hundred and twelve young
    men.

Retreating they had formed in a hollow square with their baggage for
    breastworks,
Nine hundred lives out of the surrounding enemy's nine times their
    number was the price they took in advance,
Their colonel was wounded and their ammunition gone,
They treated for an honorable capitulation, received writing and seal,
    gave up their arms, and marched back prisoners of war.

They were the glory of the race of rangers,
Matchless with a horse, a rifle, a song, a supper or a courtship,
Large, turbulent, brave, handsome, generous, proud and affectionate,
Bearded, sunburnt, dressed in the free costume of hunters,
Not a single one over thirty years of age.

The second Sunday morning they were brought out in squads and
    massacred—it was beautiful early summer,
The work commenced about five o'clock and was over by eight.

None obeyed the command to kneel,
Some made a mad and helpless rush—some stood stark and straight,
A few fell at once, shot in the temple or heart—the living and dead
    lay together,
The maimed and mangled dug in the dirt—the new-comers saw them
    there,
Some half-killed attempted to crawl away,
These were dispatched with bayonets or battered with the blunts of
    muskets,
A youth not seventeen years old seized his assassin till two more came
    to release him,
The three were all torn, and covered with the boy's blood.

At eleven o'clock began the burning of the bodies,
And that is the tale of the murder of the four hundred and twelve
    young men,
And that was a jetblack sunrise.

35
Did you read in the seabooks of the old-fashioned frigate-fight?
Did you learn who won by the light of the moon and stars?

Our foe was no skulk in his ship, I tell you,
His was the English pluck, and there is no tougher or truer, and
    never was, and never will be,
Along the lowered eve he came, horribly raking us.

We closed with him—the yards entangled—the cannon touched,
My captain lashed fast with his own hands.

We had received some eighteen-pound shots under the water,
On our lower-gun-deck two large pieces had burst at the first fire,
    killing all around and blowing up overhead.

Ten o'clock at night, and the full moon shining and the leaks on the
    gain, and five feet of water reported,
The master-at-arms loosing the prisoners confined in the after-hold to
    give them a chance for themselves.

The transit to and from the magazine was now stopped by the sentinels,
They saw so many strange faces they did not know whom to trust.

Our frigate was afire, the other asked if we demanded quarter? if our
    colors were struck and the fighting done?

I laughed content when I heard the voice of my little captain,
We have not struck, he composedly cried, We have just begun our
    part of the fighting.

Only three guns were in use,
One was directed by the captain himself against the enemy's main-mast,
Two well-served with grape and canister silenced his musketry and
    cleared his decks.

The tops alone seconded the fire of this little battery, especially the
    maintop,
They all held out bravely during the whole of the action.

Not a moment's cease,
The leaks gained fast on the pumps—the fire eats toward the
    powder-magazine,
One of the pumps was shot away—it was generally thought we were
    sinking.

Serene stood the little captain,
He was not hurried—his voice was neither high nor low,
His eyes gave more light to us than our battle-lanterns.

Toward twelve at night, there in the beams of the moon they
    surrendered to us.

36

Stretched and still lay the midnight,
Two great hulls motionless on the breast of the darkness,
Our vessel riddled and slowly sinking—preparations to pass to the
    one we had conquered,
The captain on the quarter-deck coldly giving his orders through a
    countenance white as a sheet,
Near by the corpse of the child that served in the cabin,
The dead face of an old salt with long white hair and carefully curled
    whiskers,
The flames spite of all that could be done flickering aloft and below,
The husky voices of the two or three officers yet fit for duty,
Formless stacks of bodies and bodies by themselves—dabs of flesh
    upon the masts and spars,
The cut of cordage and dangle of rigging, the slight shock of the
    soothe of waves,
Black and impassive guns, and litter of powder-parcels, and the strong
    scent,
Delicate sniffs of the sea-breeze, smells of sedgy grass and fields by the
    shore, death-messages given in charge to survivors,
The hiss of the surgeon's knife and the gnawing teeth of his saw,
The wheeze, the cluck, the swash of falling blood, the short wild
    scream, the long dull tapering groan,
These so—these irretrievable.

37

O Christ! My fit is mastering me!
Through the conquered doors they crowd. I am possessed.

I become any presence or truth of humanity here,
And see myself in prison shaped like another man,
And feel the dull unintermitted pain.

For me the keepers of convicts shoulder their carbines and keep watch,
It is I let out in the morning and barred at night.

Not a mutineer walks handcuffed to the jail, but I am handcuffed to
    him and walk by his side,
I am less the jolly one there, and more the silent one with sweat on
    my twitching lips.

Not a youngster is taken for larceny, but I go too and am tried and
    sentenced.

Not a cholera patient lies at the last gasp, but I also lie at the last gasp,
My face is ash-colored, my sinews gnarl—away from me people retreat.

Askers embody themselves in me, and I am embodied in them,
I project my hat and sit shamefaced and beg.

38
Somehow I have been stunned. Stand back!
Give me a little time beyond my cuffed head and slumbers and
    dreams and gaping,
I discover myself on a verge of the usual mistake.

That I could forget the mockers and insults!
That I could forget the trickling tears and the blows of the
    bludgeons and hammers!
That I could look with a separate look on my own crucifixion and
    bloody crowning!

I remember, I resume the overstaid fraction,

The grave of rock multiplies what has been confided to it, or to any
    graves,
The corpses rise, the gashes heal, the fastenings roll away.

I troop forth replenished with supreme power, one of an average
    unending procession,
We walk the roads of Ohio and Massachusetts and Virginia and
    Wisconsin and New York and New Orleans and Texas and
    Montreal and San Francisco and Charleston and Savannah
    and Mexico,
Inland and by the sea-coast and boundary lines, and we pass the
    boundary lines.

Our swift ordinances are on their way over the whole earth,
The blossoms we wear in our hats are the growth of two thousand years.

Eleves I salute you,
I see the approach of your numberless gangs—I see you understand
    yourselves and me,
And know that they who have eyes are divine, and the blind and lame
    are equally divine,
And that my steps drag behind yours yet go before them,
And are aware how I am with you no more than I am with everybody.

39
The friendly and flowing savage, who is he?
Is he waiting for civilization or past it and mastering it?

Is he some southwesterner raised outdoors? is he Canadian?
Is he from the Mississippi country? or from Iowa, Oregon or
    California? or from the mountains? or prairie life or bush-life?
    or from the sea?

Wherever he goes men and women accept and desire him,

They desire he should like them and touch them and speak to them
    and stay with them.

Behaviour lawless as snow-flakes, words simple as grass, uncombed
    head and laughter and naivete,
Slow-stepping feet and the common features, and the common modes
    and emanations,
They descend in new forms from the tips of his fingers,
They are wafted with the odor of his body or breath—they fly out of
    the glance of his eyes.

40

Flaunt of the sunshine I need not your bask—lie over,
You light surfaces only—I force the surfaces and the depths also.

Earth! you seem to look for something at my hands,
Say old topknot! what do you want?

Man or woman! I might tell how I like you, but cannot,
And might tell what it is in me and what it is in you, but cannot,
And might tell the pinings I have—the pulse of my nights and days.

Behold I do not give lectures or a little charity,
What I give I give out of myself.

You there, impotent, loose in the knees, open your scarfed chops till
    I blow grit within you,
Spread your palms and lift the flaps of your pockets,
I am not to be denied—I compel—I have stores plenty and to spare,
And any thing I have I bestow.

I do not ask who you are—that is not important to me,
You can do nothing and be nothing but what I will infold you.

To a drudge of the cotton-fields or emptier of privies I lean—on his
 right cheek I put the family kiss,
And in my soul I swear I never will deny him.

On women fit for conception I start bigger and nimbler babes,
This day I am jetting the stuff of far more arrogant republics.

To any one dying—thither I speed and twist the knob of the door,
Turn the bed-clothes toward the foot of the bed,
Let the physician and the priest go home.

I seize the descending man, I raise him with resistless will.

O despairer, here is my neck,
By God! you shall not go down! hang your whole weight upon me.

I dilate you with tremendous breath—I buoy you up,
Every room of the house do I fill with an armed force, lovers of me,
 bafflers of graves.

Sleep! I and they keep guard all night,
Not doubt, not decease shall dare to lay finger upon you,
I have embraced you, and henceforth possess you to myself,
And when you rise in the morning you will find what I tell you is so.

41
I am he bringing help for the sick as they pant on their backs,
And for strong upright men I bring yet more needed help.

I heard what was said of the universe,
Heard it and heard it of several thousand years,
It is middling well as far as it goes—but is that all?

Magnifying and applying come I,

Outbidding at the start the old cautious hucksters,

The most they offer for mankind and eternity less than a spirt of my own seminal wet,

Taking myself the exact dimensions of Jehovah and laying them away,

Lithographing Kronos and Zeus his son, and Hercules his grandson,

Buying drafts of Osiris and Isis and Belus and Brahma and Adonai,

In my portfolio placing Manito loose, and Allah on a leaf, and the crucifix engraved,

With Odin, and the hideous-faced Mexitli, and all idols and images,

Honestly taking them all for what they are worth, and not a cent more,

Admitting they were alive and did the work of their day,

Admitting they bore mites as for unfledged birds who have now to rise and fly and sing for themselves,

Accepting the rough deific sketches to fill out better in myself— bestowing them freely on each man and woman I see,

Discovering as much or more in a framer framing a house,

Putting higher claims for him there with his rolled-up sleeves, driving the mallet and chisel,

Not objecting to special revelations—considering a curl of smoke or a hair on the back of my hand as curious as any revelation,

Those ahold of fire-engines and hook-and-ladder ropes more to me than the gods of the antique wars,

Minding their voices' peal through the crash of destruction,

Their brawny limbs passing safe over charred laths—their white foreheads whole and unhurt out of the flames,

By the mechanic's wife with her babe at her nipple interceding for every person born,

Three scythes at harvest whizzing in a row from three lusty angels with shirts bagged out at their waists,

The snag-toothed hostler with red hair redeeming sins past and to come,

Selling all he possesses and traveling on foot to fee lawyers for his brother and sit by him while he is tried for forgery,

What was strewn in the amplest strewing the square rod about me,
    and not filling the square rod then,
The bull and the bug never worshipped half enough,
Dung and dirt more admirable than was dreamed,
The supernatural of no account—myself waiting my time to be one
    of the supremes,
The day getting ready for me when I shall do as much good as the
    best, and be as prodigious,
Guessing when I am it will not tickle me much to receive puffs out of
    pulpit or print,
By my life-lumps! becoming already a creator!
Putting myself here and now to the ambushed womb of the shadows!

42
A call in the midst of the crowd,
My own voice, orotund sweeping and final.

Come my children,
Come my boys and girls, and my women and household and intimates,
Now the performer launches his nerve—he has passed his prelude on
    the reeds within.

Easily written loose-fingered chords! I feel the thrum of their climax
    and close.

My head slues round on my neck,
Music rolls, but not from the organ, folks are around me, but they
    are no household of mine.

Ever the hard and unsunk ground,
Ever the eaters and drinkers—ever the upward and downward sun—
    ever the air and the ceaseless tides,
Ever myself and my neighbors, refreshing and wicked and real,

Ever the old inexplicable query—ever that thorned thumb—that
    breath of itches and thirsts,
Ever the vexer's hoot! hoot! till we find where the sly one hides and
    bring him forth,
Ever love—ever the sobbing liquid of life,
Ever the bandage under the chin—ever the trestles of death.

Here and there with dimes on the eyes walking,
To feed the greed of the belly the brains liberally spooning,
Tickets buying or taking or selling, but in to the feast never once
    going,
Many sweating and ploughing and thrashing, and then the chaff for
    payment receiving,
A few idly owning, and they the wheat continually claiming.

This is the city—and I am one of the citizens,
Whatever interests the rest interests me—politics, churches,
    newspapers, schools,
Benevolent societies, improvements, banks, tariffs, steam-ships,
    factories, markets,
Stocks and stores and real estate and personal estate.

They who piddle and patter here in collars and tailed coats—I am
    aware who they are—and that they are not worms or fleas,
I acknowledge the duplicates of myself under all the scrape-lipped and
    pipe-legged concealments.

The weakest and shallowest is deathless with me,
What I do and say the same waits for them,
Every thought that flounders in me the same flounders in them.

I know perfectly well my own egotism,
And know my omnivorous words, and cannot say any less,
And would fetch you whoever you are flush with myself.

My words are words of a questioning, and to indicate reality;

This printed and bound book—but the printer and the printing-
office boy?

The marriage estate and settlement—but the body and mind of the
bridegroom? also those of the bride?

The panorama of the sea—but the sea itself?

The well-taken photographs—but your wife or friend close and solid
in your arms?

The fleet of ships of the line and all the modern improvements—but
the craft and pluck of the admiral?

The dishes and fare and furniture—but the host and hostess, and the
look out of their eyes?

The sky up there—yet here or next door or across the way?

The saints and sages in history—but you yourself?

Sermons and creeds and theology—but the human brain, and what is
called reason, and what is called love, and what is called life?

43

I do not despise you priests,

My faith is the greatest of faiths and the least of faiths,

Enclosing all worship ancient and modern, and all between ancient and
modern,

Believing I shall come again upon the earth after five thousand years,

Waiting responses from oracles, honoring the gods, saluting the sun,

Making a fetish of the first rock or stump, powowing with sticks in
the circle of obis,

Helping the lama or brahmin as he trims the lamps of the idols,

Dancing yet through the streets in a phallic procession—rapt and
austere in the woods, a gymnosophist,

Drinking mead from the skull-cup—to shasta and vedas admirant—
minding the koran,

Walking the teokallis, spotted with gore from the stone and knife—
beating the serpent-skin drum,

Accepting the gospels, accepting him that was crucified, knowing
    assuredly that he is divine,
To the mass kneeling, to the puritan's prayer rising, sitting patiently
    in a pew,
Ranting and frothing in my insane crisis, waiting dead-like till my
    spirit arouses me,
Looking forth on pavement and land, and outside of pavement and
    land,
Belonging to the winders of the circuit of circuits.

One of that centripetal and centrifugal gang,
I turn and talk like a man leaving charges before a journey.

Down-hearted doubters, dull and excluded,
Frivolous sullen moping angry affected disheartened atheistical,
I know every one of you, and know the unspoken interrogatories,
By experience I know them.

How the flukes splash!
How they contort rapid as lightning, with spasms and spouts of blood!

Be at peace bloody flukes of doubters and sullen mopers,
I take my place among you as much as among any,
The past is the push of you and me and all precisely the same,
And the day and night are for you and me and all,
And what is yet untried and afterward is for you and me and all.

I do not know what is untried and afterward,
But I know it is sure and alive and sufficient.

Each who passes is considered, and each who stops is considered, and
    not a single one can it fail.

It cannot fail the young man who died and was buried,

Nor the young woman who died and was put by his side,

Nor the little child that peeped in at the door and then drew back and was never seen again,

Nor the old man who has lived without purpose, and feels it with bitterness worse than gall,

Nor him in the poor house tubercled by rum and the bad disorder,

Nor the numberless slaughtered and wrecked—nor the brutish koboo, called the ordure of humanity,

Nor the sacs merely floating with open mouths for food to slip in,

Nor any thing in the earth, or down in the oldest graves of the earth,

Nor any thing in the myriads of spheres, nor one of the myriads of myriads that inhabit them,

Nor the present, nor the least wisp that is known.

44
It is time to explain myself—let us stand up.

What is known I strip away—I launch all men and women forward with me into the unknown.

The clock indicates the moment—but what does eternity indicate?

Eternity lies in bottomless reservoirs—its buckets are rising forever and ever,
They pour and they pour and they exhale away.

We have thus far exhausted trillions of winters and summers,
There are trillions ahead, and trillions ahead of them.

Births have brought us richness and variety,
And other births will bring us richness and variety.

I do not call one greater and one smaller,
That which fills its period and place is equal to any.

Were mankind murderous or jealous upon you my brother or my
    sister?
I am sorry for you—they are not murderous or jealous upon me,
All has been gentle with me—I keep no account with lamentation,
What have I to do with lamentation?

I am an acme of things accomplished, and I an encloser of things to be.

My feet strike an apex of the apices of the stairs,
On every step bunches of ages, and larger bunches between the steps,
All below duly traveled, and still I mount and mount.

Rise after rise bow the phantoms behind me,
Afar down I see the huge first Nothing, the vapor from the nostrils
    of death,
I know I was even there, I waited unseen and always,
And slept while God carried me through the lethargic mist,
And took my time, and took no hurt from the fœtid carbon.

Long I was hugged close—long and long.

Immense have been the preparations for me,
Faithful and friendly the arms that have helped me.

Cycles ferried my cradle, rowing and rowing like cheerful boatmen,
For room to me stars kept aside in their own rings,
They sent influences to look after what was to hold me.

Before I was born out of my mother generations guided me,
My embryo has never been torpid—nothing could overlay it,
For it the nebula cohered to an orb—the long slow strata piled to
    rest it on—vast vegetables gave it sustenance,
Monstrous sauroids transported it in their mouths and deposited it
    with care.

All forces have been steadily employed to complete and delight me,
Now I stand on this spot with my soul.

45

Span of youth! ever-pushed elasticity! Manhood balanced and
    florid and full.

My lovers suffocate me!
Crowding my lips, and thick in the pores of my skin,
Jostling me through streets and public halls—coming naked to me at
    night,
Crying by day Ahoy from the rocks of the river—swinging and
    chirping over my head,
Calling my name from flowerbeds or vines or tangled underbrush,
Or while I swim in the bath, or drink from the pump at the corner—
    or the curtain is down at the opera, or I glimpse at a woman's
    face in the railroad car,
Lighting on every moment of my life,
Bussing my body with soft and balsamic busses,
Noiselessly passing handfuls out of their hearts and giving them to be
    mine.

Old age superbly rising! ineffable grace of dying days!

Every condition promulges not only itself—it promulges what grows
    after and out of itself,
And the dark hush promulges as much as any.

I open my scuttle at night and see the far-sprinkled systems,
And all I see, multiplied as high as I can cipher, edge but the rim of
    the farther systems.

Wider and wider they spread, expanding and always expanding,
Outward and outward and forever outward.

My sun has his sun, and round him obediently wheels,
He joins with his partners a group of superior circuit,
And greater sets follow, making specks of the greatest inside them.

There is no stoppage, and never can be stoppage,
If I and you and the worlds and all beneath or upon their surfaces, and
    all the palpable life, were this moment reduced back to a pallid
    float, it would not avail in the long run,
We should surely bring up again where we now stand,
And as surely go as much farther, and then farther and farther.

A few quadrillions of eras, a few octillions of cubic leagues, do not
    hazard the span, or make it impatient,
They are but parts — any thing is but a part.

See ever so far, there is limitless space outside of that,
Count ever so much, there is limitless time around that.

Our rendezvous is fitly appointed, God will be there and wait till we
    come.

46

I know I have the best of time and space, and that I was never
    measured, and never will be measured.

I tramp a perpetual journey,
My signs are a rain-proof coat and good shoes and a staff cut from
    the woods,
No friend of mine takes his ease in my chair,
I have no chair, nor church nor philosophy,
I lead no man to a dinner-table or library or exchange,
But each man and each woman of you I lead upon a knoll,
My left hand hooking you round the waist,

My right hand pointing to landscapes of continents, and the public
    road.

Not I, not any one else can travel that road for you,
You must travel it for yourself.

It is not far—it is within reach,
Perhaps you have been on it since you were born, and did not know,
Perhaps it is every where on water and on land.

Shoulder your duds, and I will mine, and let us hasten forth,
Wonderful cities and free nations we shall fetch as we go.

If you tire, give me both burdens, and rest the chuff of your hand
    on my hip,
And in due time you shall repay the same service to me,
For after we start we never lie by again.

This day before dawn I ascended a hill and looked at the crowded
    heaven,
And I said to my spirit, When we become the enfolders of those orbs
    and the pleasure and knowledge of every thing in them, shall we
    be filled and satisfied then?
And my spirit said No, we but level that lift to pass and continue
    beyond.

You are also asking me questions, and I hear you,
I answer that I cannot answer—you must find out for yourself.

Sit awhile wayfarer,
Here are biscuits to eat and here is milk to drink,
But as soon as you sleep and renew yourself in sweet clothes I kiss you
    with a goodbye kiss and open the gate for your egress hence.

Long enough have you dreamed contemptible dreams,
Now I wash the gum from your eyes,
You must habit yourself to the dazzle of the light and of every
        moment of your life.

Long have you timidly waded, holding a plank by the shore,
Now I will you to be a bold swimmer,
To jump off in the midst of the sea, and rise again and nod to me and
        shout, and laughingly dash with your hair.

47

I am the teacher of athletes,
He that by me spreads a wider breast than my own proves the
        width of my own,
He most honors my style who learns under it to destroy the teacher.

The boy I love, the same becomes a man not through derived power
        but in his own right,
Wicked, rather than virtuous out of conformity or fear,
Fond of his sweetheart, relishing well his steak,
Unrequited love or a slight cutting him worse than a wound cuts,
First rate to ride, to fight, to hit the bull's eye, to sail a skiff, to sing
        a song or play on the banjo,
Preferring scars and faces pitted with smallpox over all latherers and
        those that keep out of the sun.

I teach straying from me, yet who can stray from me?
I follow you whoever you are from the present hour,
My words itch at your eyes till you understand them.

I do not say these things for a dollar, or to fill up the time while I
        wait for a boat,
It is you talking just as much as myself—I act as the tongue of you,
It was tied in your mouth, in mine it begins to be loosened.

I swear I will never mention love or death inside a house,
And I swear I never will translate myself at all, only to him or her who
   privately stays with me in the open air.

If you would understand me go to the heights or water-shore,
The nearest gnat is an explanation and a drop or the motion of
   waves a key,
The maul the oar and the handsaw second my words.

No shuttered room or school can commune with me,
But roughs and little children better than they.

The young mechanic is closest to me—he knows me pretty well,
The woodman that takes his axe and jug with him shall take me with
   him all day,
The farmboy ploughing in the field feels good at the sound of my
   voice,
In vessels that sail my words must sail—I go with fishermen and
   seamen, and love them,
My face rubs to the hunter's face when he lies down alone in his
   blanket,
The driver thinking of me does not mind the jolt of his wagon,
The young mother and old mother shall comprehend me,
The girl and the wife rest the needle a moment and forget where
   they are,
They and all would resume what I have told them.

48

I have said that the soul is not more than the body,
And I have said that the body is not more than the soul,
And nothing, not God, is greater to one than one's-self is,
And whoever walks a furlong without sympathy walks to his own
   funeral, dressed in his shroud,
And I or you pocketless of a dime may purchase the pick of the earth,

And to glance with an eye or show a bean in its pod confounds the
learning of all times,
And there is no trade or employment but the young man following
it may become a hero,
And there is no object so soft but it makes a hub for the wheeled
universe,
And any man or woman shall stand cool and supercilious before a
million universes.

And I call to mankind, Be not curious about God,
For I who am curious about each am not curious about God,
No array of terms can say how much I am at peace about God and
about death.

I hear and behold God in every object, yet I understand God not in
the least,
Nor do I understand who there can be more wonderful than myself.

Why should I wish to see God better than this day?
I see something of God each hour of the twenty-four, and each
moment then,
In the faces of men and women I see God, and in my own face in the
glass,
I find letters from God dropped in the street, and every one is signed
by God's name,
And I leave them where they are, for I know that others will punctually
come forever and ever.

49
And as to you death, and you bitter hug of mortality, it is idle to
try to alarm me.

To his work without flinching the accoucheur comes,
I see the elderhand pressing receiving supporting,

I recline by the sills of the exquisite flexible doors, and mark the
outlet, and mark the relief and escape.

And as to you corpse I think you are good manure, but that does
not offend me,
I smell the white roses sweet-scented and growing,
I reach to the leafy lips—I reach to the polished breasts of melons.

And as to you life, I reckon you are the leavings of many deaths,
No doubt I have died myself ten thousand times before.

I hear you whispering there O stars of heaven,
O sun! O grass of graves! O perpetual transfers and promotions!
if you do not say anything how can I say anything?

Of the turbid pool that lies in the autumn forest,
Of the moon that descends the steeps of the soughing twilight,
Toss, sparkles of day and dusk! toss on the black stems that decay
in the muck,
Toss to the moaning gibberish of the dry limbs.

I ascend from the moon, I ascend from the night,
And perceive of the ghastly glitter the sunbeams reflected,
And debouch to the steady and central from the offspring great or
small.

50
There is that in me—I do not know what it is—but I know it is
in me.

Wrenched and sweaty—calm and cool then my body becomes, I
sleep—I sleep long.

I do not know it—it is without name—it is a word unsaid,
It is not in any dictionary or utterance or symbol.

Something it swings on more than the earth I swing on,
To it the creation is the friend whose embracing awakes me.

Perhaps I might tell more. Outlines! I plead for my brothers and
   sisters.

Do you see O my brothers and sisters?
It is not chaos or death—it is form and union and plan—it is
   eternal life—it is happiness.

51
The past and present wilt—I have filled them and emptied them,
And proceed to fill my next fold of the future.

Listener up there! what have you to confide to me?
Look in my face while I snuff the sidle of evening,
Talk honestly, for no one else hears you, and I stay only a minute
   longer.

Do I contradict myself?
Very well then, I contradict myself,
I am large—I contain multitudes.

I concentrate toward them that are nigh—I wait on the door-slab.

Who has done his day's work and will soonest be through with his
   supper?
Who wishes to walk with me?

Will you speak before I am gone? Will you prove already too late?

52
The spotted hawk swoops by and accuses me—he complains of my
   gab and my loitering.

I too am not a bit tamed—I too am untranslatable,
I sound my barbaric yawp over the roofs of the world.

The last scud of day holds back for me,
It flings my likeness after the rest and true as any on the shadowed
    wilds,
It coaxes me to the vapor and the dusk.

I depart as air—I shake my white locks at the runaway sun,
I effuse my flesh in eddies and drift it in lacy jags.

I bequeath myself to the dirt to grow from the grass I love,
If you want me again look for me under your boot-soles.

You will hardly know who I am or what I mean,
But I shall be good health to you nevertheless,
And filter and fibre your blood.

Failing to fetch me at first keep encouraged,
Missing me one place search another,
I stop some where waiting for you.

Sleep-Chasings

1
I wander all night in my vision,
Stepping with light feet, swiftly and noiselessly stepping and
        stopping,
Bending with open eyes over the shut eyes of sleepers,
Wandering and confused, lost to myself, ill-assorted, contradictory,
Pausing and gazing and bending and stopping.

How solemn they look there, stretched and still,
How quiet they breathe, the little children in their cradles.

The wretched features of ennuyees, the white features of corpses,
    the livid faces of drunkards, the sick-gray faces of onanists,
The gashed bodies on battlefields, the insane in their strong-doored
    rooms, the sacred idiots,
The newborn emerging from gates and the dying emerging from gates,
The night pervades them and enfolds them.

The married couple sleep calmly in their bed, he with his palm on the
    hip of the wife, and she with her palm on the hip of the husband,
The sisters sleep lovingly side by side in their bed,
The men sleep lovingly side by side in theirs,
And the mother sleeps, with her little child carefully wrapped.

The blind sleep, and the deaf and dumb sleep,
The prisoner sleeps well in the prison—the runaway son sleeps,
The murderer that is to be hung next day—how does he sleep?
And the murdered person—how does he sleep?

The female that loves unrequited sleeps,
And the male that loves unrequited sleeps,
The head of the money-maker that plotted all day sleeps,
And the enraged and treacherous dispositions—all, all sleep.

I stand in the dark with drooping eyes by the worst-suffering and
    restless,
I pass my hands soothingly to and fro a few inches from them,
The restless sink in their beds—they fitfully sleep.

The earth recedes from me into the night,
I saw that it was beautiful, and I see that what is not the earth is
    beautiful.

I go from bedside to bedside—I sleep close with the other sleepers,
    each in turn,

I dream in my dream all the dreams of the other dreamers,
And I become the other dreamers.

I am a dance—play up there! the fit is whirling me fast.

I am the everlaughing—it is new moon and twilight,
I see the hiding of douceurs—I see nimble ghosts whichever way I
  look,
Cache, and cache again, deep in the ground and sea, and where it is
  neither ground or sea.

Well do they do their jobs, those journeymen divine,
Only from me can they hide nothing, and would not if they could,
I reckon I am their boss, and they make me a pet besides,
And surround me and lead me, and run ahead when I walk,
To lift their cunning covers, to signify me with stretched arms, and
  resume the way;
Onward we move! a gay gang of blackguards! with mirth-shouting
  music and wild-flapping pennants of joy!

I am the actor and the actress, the voter, the politician,
The emigrant and the exile, the criminal that stood in the box,
He who has been famous, and he who shall be famous after to-day,
The stammerer, the well-formed person, the wasted or feeble person.

I am she who adorned herself and folded her hair expectantly,
My truant lover has come, and it is dark.

Double yourself and receive me darkness,
Receive me and my lover too—he will not let me go without him.

I roll myself upon you as upon a bed—I resign myself to the dusk.

He whom I call answers me and takes the place of my lover,
He rises with me silently from the bed.

Darkness you are gentler than my lover—his flesh was sweaty and
    panting,
I feel the hot moisture yet that he left me.

My hands are spread forth, I pass them in all directions,
I would sound up the shadowy shore to which you are journeying.

Be careful, darkness—already, what was it touched me?
I thought my lover had gone, else darkness and he are one,
I hear the heart-beat—I follow, I fade away.

O hot-cheeked and blushing! O foolish hectic!
O for pity's sake, no one must see me now! my clothes were stolen
    while I was abed,
Now I am thrust forth, where shall I run?

Pier that I saw dimly last night when I looked from the windows,
Pier out from the main, let me catch myself with you and stay—I will
    not chafe you,
I feel ashamed to go naked about the world.
I am curious to know where my feet stand—and what is this
    flooding me, childhood or manhood—and the hunger that
    crosses the bridge between.

The cloth laps a first sweet eating and drinking,
Laps life-swelling yolks—laps ear of rose-corn, milky and just ripened,
The white teeth stay, and the boss-tooth advances in darkness,
And liquor is spilled on lips and bosoms by touching glasses, and the
    best liquor afterward.

2
I descend my western course, my sinews are flaccid,
Perfume and youth course through me, and I am their wake.

It is my face yellow and wrinkled instead of the old woman's,
I sit low in a straw-bottom chair and carefully darn my grandson's
stockings.

It is I too, the sleepless widow looking out on the winter midnight,
I see the sparkles of starshine on the icy and pallid earth.

A shroud I see—and I am the shroud, I wrap a body and lie in the
coffin,
It is dark here under-ground—it is not evil or pain here—it is blank
here, for reasons.

It seems to me that everything in the light and air ought to be happy,
Whoever is not in his coffin and the dark grave, let him know he has
enough.

3

I see a beautiful gigantic swimmer swimming naked through the
eddies of the sea,
His brown hair lies close and even to his head—he strikes out with
courageous arms, he urges himself with his legs.

I see his white body—I see his undaunted eyes,
I hate the swift-running eddies that would dash him headforemost on
the rocks.

What are you doing you ruffianly red-trickled waves?
Will you kill the courageous giant? Will you kill him in the prime
of his middle age?

Steady and long he struggles,
He is baffled and banged and bruised—he holds out while his
strength holds out,

The slapping eddies are spotted with his blood—they bear him
    away—they roll him and swing him and turn him,
His beautiful body is borne in the circling eddies, it is continually
    bruised on rocks,
Swiftly and out of sight is borne the brave corpse.

4

I turn but do not extricate myself,
Confused, a past-reading, another, but with darkness yet.

The beach is cut by the razory ice-wind—the wreck guns sound,
The tempest lulls and the moon comes floundering through the drifts.

I look where the ship helplessly heads end on—I hear the burst as
    she strikes—I hear the howls of dismay, they grow fainter and
    fainter.

I cannot aid with my wringing fingers,
I can but rush to the surf and let it drench me and freeze upon me.

I search with the crowd—not one of the company is washed to us alive,
In the morning I help pick up the dead and lay them in rows in a barn.

5

Now of the old war-days, the defeat at Brooklyn,
Washington stands inside the lines—he stands on the entrenched hills
    amid a crowd of officers,
His face is cold and damp—he cannot repress the weeping drops,
    he lifts the glass perpetually to his eyes—the color is blanched
    from his cheeks,
He sees the slaughter of the southern braves confided to him by their
    parents.

The same at last and at last when peace is declared,

He stands in the room of the old tavern — the well-beloved soldiers
    all pass through.

The officers speechless and slow draw near in their turns,
The chief encircles their necks with his arm and kisses them on the
    cheek,
He kisses lightly the wet cheeks one after another, he shakes hands
    and bids goodbye to the army.

6
Now I tell what my mother told me today as we sat at dinner
    together,
Of when she was a nearly grown girl living home with her parents
    on the old homestead.

A red squaw came one breakfast-time to the old homestead,
On her back she carried a bundle of rushes for rush-bottoming chairs;
Her hair straight shiny coarse black and profuse half-enveloped her face,
Her step was free and elastic, her voice sounded exquisitely as she
    spoke.

My mother looked in delight and amazement at the stranger,
She looked at the freshness of her tall-borne face and full and pliant
    limbs,
The more she looked upon her she loved her,
Never before had she seen such wonderful beauty and purity;
She made her sit on a bench by the jamb of the fireplace, she
    cooked food for her,
She had no work to give her but she gave her remembrance and
    fondness.

The red squaw staid all the forenoon, and toward the middle of the
    afternoon she went away,
O my mother was loth to have her go away,

All the week she thought of her—she watched for her many a month,
She remembered her many a winter and many a summer,
But the red squaw never came nor was heard of there again.

Now Lucifer was not dead—or if he was I am his sorrowful terrible
heir,
I have been wronged—I am oppressed—I hate him that oppresses me,
I will either destroy him, or he shall release me.

Damn him! how he does defile me,
How he informs against my brother and sister and takes pay for their
blood,
How he laughs when I look down the bend after the steamboat that
carries away my woman.

Now the vast dusk bulk that is the whale's bulk, it seems mine,
Warily, sportsman! though I lie so sleepy and sluggish, my tap is death.

7
A show of the summer softness, a contact of something unseen, an
amour of the light and air,
I am jealous and overwhelmed with friendliness,
And will go gallivant with the light and the air myself,
And have an unseen something to be in contact with them also.

O love and summer! you are in the dreams and in me,
Autumn and winter are in the dreams—the farmer goes with his thrift,
The droves and crops increase, the barns are well-filled.

Elements merge in the night—ships make tacks in the dreams the
sailor sails—the exile returns home,
The fugitive returns unharmed—the immigrant is back beyond
months and years,

The poor Irishman lives in the simple house of his childhood, with the well-known neighbors and faces,
They warmly welcome him—he is barefoot again, he forgets he is well off;
The Dutchman voyages home, and the Scotchman and Welshman voyage home, and the native of the Mediterranean voyages home,
To every port of England and France and Spain enter well-filled ships,
The Swiss foots it toward his hills—the Prussian goes his way, and the Hungarian his way, and the Pole goes his way,
The Swede returns, and the Dane and Norwegian return.

The homeward bound and the outward bound,
The beautiful lost swimmer, the ennuyee, the onanist, the female that loves unrequited, the money-maker,
The actor and actress, those through with their parts and those waiting to commence,
The affectionate boy, the husband and wife, the voter, the nominee that is chosen and the nominee that has failed,
The great already known, and the great anytime after to day,
The stammerer, the sick, the perfect-formed, the homely,
The criminal that stood in the box, the judge that sat and sentenced him, the fluent lawyers, the jury, the audience,
The laugher and weeper, the dancer, the midnight widow, the red squaw,
The consumptive, the erysipalite, the idiot, he that is wronged,
The antipodes, and every one between this and them in the dark,
I swear they are averaged now—one is no better than the other,
The night and sleep have likened them and restored them.

I swear they are all beautiful,
Every one that sleeps is beautiful—every thing in the dim night is beautiful,
The wildest and bloodiest is over and all is peace.

Peace is always beautiful,
The myth of heaven indicates peace and night.

The myth of heaven indicates the soul,
The soul is always beautiful—it appears more or it appears less—it
    comes or lags behind,
It comes from its embowered garden and looks pleasantly on itself
    and encloses the world,
Perfect and clean the genitals previously jetting, and perfect and clean
    the womb cohering,
The head well-grown and proportioned and plumb, and the bowels and
    joints proportioned and plumb.

The soul is always beautiful,
The universe is duly in order, every thing is in its place,
What is arrived is in its place, and what waits is in its place,
The twisted skull waits, the watery or rotten blood waits,
The child of the glutton or venerealee waits long, and the child of the
    drunkard waits long, and the drunkard himself waits long,
The sleepers that lived and died wait—the far advanced are to go
    on in their turns, and the far behind are to go on in their turns,
The diverse shall be no less diverse, but they shall flow and unite—
    they unite now.

8
The sleepers are very beautiful as they lie unclothed,
They flow hand in hand over the whole earth from east to west as
    they lie unclothed,
The Asiatic and African are hand in hand—the European and American
    are hand in hand,
Learned and unlearned are hand in hand—and male and female are
    hand in hand,
The bare arm of the girl crosses the bare breast of her lover—they
    press close without lust—his lips press her neck,
The father holds his grown or ungrown son in his arms with

measureless love, and the son holds the father in his arms with
measureless love,

The white hair of the mother shines on the white wrist of the daughter,

The breath of the boy goes with the breath of the man, friend is
inarmed by friend,

The scholar kisses the teacher and the teacher kisses the scholar—the
wronged is made right,

The call of the slave is one with the master's call, and the master
salutes the slave,

The felon steps forth from the prison—the insane becomes sane—the
suffering of sick persons is relieved,

The sweatings and fevers stop, the throat that was unsound is sound,
the lungs of the consumptive are resumed, the poor distressed
head is free,

The joints of the rheumatic move as smoothly as ever, and smoother
than ever,

Stiflings and passages open—the paralysed become supple,

The swelled and convulsed and congested awake to themselves in
condition,

They pass the invigoration of the night and the chemistry of the
night and awake.

I too pass from the night,
I stay awhile away O night, but I return to you again and love you.

Why should I be afraid to trust myself to you?
I am not afraid, I have been well brought forward by you,
I love the rich running day, but I do not desert her in whom I lay so
long,
I know not how I came of you, and I know not where I go with you—
but I know I came well and shall go well.

I will stop only a time with the night, and rise betimes,
I will duly pass the day O my mother and duly return to you.

Poem of the Body

1

The bodies of men and women engirth me, and I engirth them,
They will not let me off nor I them till I go with them and respond
    to them and love them.

Was it doubted if those who corrupt their own live bodies conceal
    themselves?
And if those who defile the living are as bad as they who defile the
    dead?

2

The expression of the body of man or woman balks account,
The male is perfect and that of the female is perfect.

The expression of a well-made man appears not only in his face,
It is in his limbs and joints also, it is curiously in the joints of his
    hips and wrists,
It is in his walk, the carriage of his neck, the flex of his waist and
    knees—dress does not hide him,
The strong sweet supple quality he has strikes through the cotton and
    flannel,
To see him pass conveys as much as the best poem, perhaps more,
You linger to see his back and the back of his neck and shoulder-side.

The sprawl and fulness of babes, the bosoms and heads of women,
    the folds of their dress, their style as we pass in the street, the
    contour of their shape downwards,
The swimmer naked in the swimming-bath, seen as he swims through
    the salt transparent green-shine, or lies on his back and rolls silently
    with the heave of the water,
Framers bare-armed framing a house, hoisting the beams in their places,
    or using the mallet and mortising-chisel,

The bending forward and backward of rowers in row-boats—the
    horseman in his saddle,
Girls and mothers and housekeepers in all their exquisite offices,
The group of laborers seated at noon-time with their open dinner-kettles,
    and their wives waiting,
The female soothing a child—the farmer's daughter in the garden or
    cow-yard,
The young fellow hoeing corn—the sleigh-driver guiding his six horses
    through the crowd,
The wrestle of wrestlers, two apprentice-boys, quite grown, lusty,
    good-natured, native-born, out on the vacant lot at sun-down
    after work,
The coats vests and caps thrown down, the embrace of love and
    resistance,
The upper-hold and under-hold—the hair rumpled over and blinding
    the eyes,
The march of firemen in their own costumes—the play of the masculine
    muscle through clean-setting trowsers and waist-straps,
The slow return from the fire, the pause when the bell strikes
    suddenly again—the listening on the alert,
The natural perfect and varied attitudes—the bent head, the curved
    neck, the counting:
Such-like I love—I loosen myself and pass freely—and am at the
    mother's breast with the little child,
And swim with the swimmer, and wrestle with the wrestlers, and
    march in line with the firemen, and pause and listen and count.

3

I knew a man—he was a common farmer—he was the father of
    five sons—and in them were the fathers of sons—and in them
    were the fathers of sons.

This man was a wonderful vigor and calmness and beauty of person,
The shape of his head, the richness and breadth of his manners, the

pale yellow and white of his hair and beard, the immeasurable
    meaning of his black eyes,
These I used to go and visit him to see—he was wise also,
He was six feet tall—he was over eighty years old—his sons were
    massive clean bearded tan-faced and handsome,
They and his daughters loved him—all who saw him loved him—
    they did not love him by allowance—they loved him with
    personal love,
He drank water only—the blood showed like scarlet through the
    clear-brown skin of his face,
He was a frequent gunner and fisher—he sailed his boat himself—he
    had a fine one presented to him by a ship-joiner—he had fowling-
    pieces, presented to him by men that loved him,
When he went with his five sons and many grand-sons to hunt or fish
    you would pick him out as the most beautiful and vigorous of
    the gang,
You would wish long and long to be with him—you would wish to
    sit by him in the boat that you and he might touch each other.

4

I have perceived that to be with those I like is enough,
To stop in company with the rest at evening is enough,
To be surrounded by beautiful curious breathing laughing flesh is
    enough,
To pass among them, to touch any one, to rest my arm ever so lightly
    round his or her neck for a moment—what is this then?

I do not ask any more delight—I swim in it as in a sea.

There is something in staying close to men and women and looking
    on them and in the contact and odor of them that pleases the
    soul well,
All things please the soul, but these please the soul well.

5

This is the female form,

A divine nimbus exhales from it from head to foot,

It attracts with fierce undeniable attraction,

I am drawn by its breath as if I were no more than a helpless vapor—all falls aside but myself and it,

Books, art, religion, time, the visible and solid earth, the atmosphere and the fringed clouds, what was expected of heaven or feared of hell are now consumed,

Mad filaments, ungovernable shoots play out of it, the response likewise ungovernable,

Hair, bosom, hips, bend of legs, negligent falling hands—all diffused—mine too diffused,

Ebb stung by the flow, and flow stung by the ebb—love-flesh swelling and deliciously aching,

Limitless limpid jets of love hot and enormous, quivering jelly of love, white-blow and delirious juice,

Bridegroom night of love working surely and softly into the prostrate dawn,

Undulating into the willing and yielding day,

Lost in the cleave of the clasping and sweet-fleshed day.

This is the nucleus—after the child is born of woman the man is born of woman,

This is the bath of birth—this is the merge of small and large and the outlet again.

Be not ashamed women—your privilege encloses the rest, it is the exit of the rest,

You are the gates of the body and you are the gates of the soul.

The female contains all qualities and tempers them—she is in her place—she moves with perfect balance,

She is all things duly veiled—she is both passive and active—she is to
conceive daughters as well as sons and sons as well as daughters.

As I see my soul reflected in nature, as I see through a mist one with
inexpressible completeness and beauty, see the bent head and
arms folded over the breast—the female I see.

6

The male is not less the soul, nor more—he too is in his place,
He too is all qualities—he is action and power—the flush of the
known universe is in him,
Scorn becomes him well and appetite and defiance become him well,
The fiercest largest passions, a bliss that is utmost and sorrow that is
utmost become him well—pride is for him,
The full-spread pride of man is calming and excellent to the soul,
Knowledge becomes him—he likes it always—he brings everything
to the test of himself,
Whatever the survey, whatever the sea and the sail, he strikes
soundings at last only here,
Where else does he strike soundings except here?

The man's body is sacred and the woman's body is sacred, it is no
matter who,
Is it a slave? Is it one of the dull-faced immigrants just landed on the
wharf?

Each belongs here or anywhere just as much as the well-off—just as
much as you,
Each has his or her place in the procession.

All is a procession,
The universe is a procession with measured and perfect motion.

Do you know so much yourself that you call the slave or the dull-face
ignorant?
Do you suppose you have a right to a good sight, and he or she has
no right to a sight?
Do you think matter has cohered together from its diffused float, and
the soil is on the surface and water runs and vegetation sprouts
for you only, and not for him and her?

7
A slave at auction!
I help the auctioneer—the sloven does not half know his business.

Gentlemen look on this curious creature,
Whatever the bids of the bidders they cannot be high enough for him,
For him the globe lay preparing quintillions of years without one
animal or plant,
For him the revolving cycles truly and steadily rolled.

In this head the all-baffling brain,
In it and below it the making of the attributes of heroes.

Examine these limbs, red black or white—they are very cunning in
tendon and nerve,
They shall be script that you may see them.

Exquisite senses, life-lit eyes, pluck, volition,
Flakes of breast-muscle, pliant backbone and neck, flesh not flabby,
good-sized arms and legs,
And wonders within there yet.

Within there runs his blood, the same old blood, the same red
running blood,

There swells and jets his heart—there all passions and desires—all
    reachings and aspirations,
Do you think they are not there because they are not expressed in
    parlors and lecture-rooms?

This is not only one man, he is the father of those who shall be fathers
    in their turns,
In him the start of populous states and rich republics,
Of him countless immortal lives with countless embodiments and
    enjoyments.

How do you know who shall come from the offspring of his offspring
    through the centuries?
Who might you find you have come from yourself if you could trace
    back through the centuries?

8

A woman at auction,
She too is not only herself—she is the teeming mother of mothers,
She is the bearer of them that shall grow and be mates to the mothers.

Her daughters or their daughters' daughters—who knows who shall
    mate with them?
Who knows through the centuries what heroes may come from them?

In them and of them natal love—in them the divine mystery—the same
    old beautiful mystery.

Have you ever loved a woman?
Your mother—is she living? have you been much with her? and has
    she been much with you?
Do you not see that these are exactly the same to all in all nations and
    times all over the earth?

If life and the soul are sacred the human body is sacred,
And the glory and sweet of a man is the token of manhood untainted,
And in man or woman a clean strong firm-fibred body is beautiful as
the most beautiful face.

Have you seen the fool that corrupted his own live body? or the fool
that corrupted her own live body?
For they do not conceal themselves, and cannot conceal themselves.

Who degrades or defiles the living human body is cursed,
Who degrades or defiles the body of the dead is not more cursed.

9

O my body! I dare not desert the likes of you in other men and
women, nor the likes of the parts of you;
I believe the likes of you are to stand or fall with the likes of the soul,
(and that they are the soul,)
I believe the likes of you shall stand or fall with my poems—and that
they are poems,
Man's, woman's, child's, youth's, wife's, husband's, mother's,
father's, young man's, young woman's poems,
Head, neck, hair, ears, drop and tympan of the ears,
Eyes, eye-fringes, iris of the eye, eye-brows, and the waking or
sleeping of the lids,
Mouth, tongue, lips, teeth, roof of the mouth, jaws, and the
jaw-hinges,
Nose, nostrils of the nose, and the partition,
Cheeks, temples, forehead, chin, throat, back of the neck, neck-slue,
Strong shoulders, manly beard, scapula, hind-shoulders, and the
ample side-round of the chest,
Upper-arm, arm-pit, elbow-socket, lower-arm, arm-sinews,
arm-bones,
Wrist and wrist-joints, hand, palm, knuckles, thumb, fore-finger,
finger-balls, finger-joints, finger-nails,

Broad breast-front, curling hair of the breast, breast-bone, breast-side,
Ribs, belly, back-bone, joints of the back-bone,
Hips, hip-sockets, hip-strength, inward and outward round,
    man-balls, man-root,
Strong set of thighs, well carrying the trunk above,
Leg-fibres, knee, knee-pan, upper-leg, under-leg,
Ankles, instep, foot-ball, toes, toe-joints, the heel,
All attitudes, all the shapeliness, all the belongings of my or your body,
    or of any one's body, male or female,
The lung-sponges, the stomach-sac, the bowels sweet and clean,
The brain in its folds inside the skull-frame,
Sympathies, heart-valves, palate-valves, sexuality, maternity,
Womanhood, and all that is a woman—and the man that comes from
    woman,
The womb, the teats, nipples, breast-milk, tears, laughter, weeping,
    love-looks, love-perturbations and risings,
The voice, articulation, language, whispering, shouting aloud,
Food, drink, pulse, digestion, sweat, sleep, walking, swimming,
Poise on the hips, leaping, reclining, embracing, arm-curving, and
    tightening,
The continual changes of the flex of the mouth, and around the eyes,
The skin, the sun-burnt shade, freckles, hair,
The curious sympathy one feels, when feeling with the hand the
    naked meat of his own body, or another person's body,
The circling rivers, the breath, and breathing it in and out,
The beauty of the waist, and thence of the hips, and thence downward
    toward the knees,
The thin red jellies within you, or within me—the bones, and the
    marrow in the bones,
The exquisite realization of health,
O I think now these are not the parts and poems of the body only,
    but of the soul,
O I think these are the soul!

There Was a Child Went Forth

There was a child went forth every day,
And the first object he looked upon, that object he became,
And that object became part of him for the day or a certain part of
    the day, or for many years or stretching cycles of years.

The early lilacs became part of this child,
And grass, and white and red morning-glories, and white and red
    clover, and the song of the phœbe-bird,
And the March-born lambs, and the sow's pink-faint litter, and the
    mare's foal, and the cow's calf, and the noisy brood of the
    barnyard or by the mire of the pond-side, and the fish suspending
    themselves so curiously below there, and the beautiful curious
    liquid, and the water-plants with their graceful flat heads, all
    became part of him.

And the field-sprouts of April and May became part of him,
    winter-grain sprouts, and those of the light-yellow corn, and
    of the esculent roots of the garden,
And the apple-trees covered with blossoms, and the fruit afterward,
    and wood-berries, and the commonest weeds by the road,
And the old drunkard staggering home from the outhouse of the
    tavern whence he had lately risen,
And the schoolmistress that passed on her way to the school, and the
    friendly boys that passed, and the quarrelsome boys, and the tidy
    and fresh-cheeked girls, and the barefoot negro boy and girl,
And all the changes of city and country wherever he went.

His own parents, he that had propelled the father-stuff at night and
    fathered him, and she that conceived him in her womb and
    birthed him, they gave this child more of themselves than that,
They gave him afterward every day—they and of them became part
    of him.

The mother at home quietly placing the dishes on the supper-table,
The mother with mild words—clean her cap and gown, a wholesome
    odor falling off her person and clothes as she walks by,
The father, strong, self-sufficient, manly, mean, angered, unjust,
The blow, the quick loud word, the tight bargain, the crafty lure,
The family usages, the language, the company, the furniture—the
    yearning and swelling heart,
Affection that will not be gainsayed—the sense of what is real—the
    thought if after all it should prove unreal,
The doubts of day-time and the doubts of night-time—the curious
    whether and how,
Whether that which appears so is so, or is it all flashes and specks?
Men and women crowding fast in the streets—if they are not flashes
    and specks what are they?
The streets themselves, and the facades of houses, the goods in the
    windows,
Vehicles, teams, the tiered wharves—and the huge crossing at the ferries,
The village on the highland seen from afar at sunset—the river between,
Shadows, aureola and mist, light falling on roofs and gables of white
    or brown, three miles off,
The schooner near by sleepily dropping down the tide—the little boat
    slack-towed astern,
The hurrying tumbling waves and quick-broken crests and slapping,
The strata of colored clouds, the long bar of maroon-tint away solitary
    by itself—the spread of purity it lies motionless in,
The horizon's edge, the flying sea-crow, the fragrance of saltmarsh
    and shore mud,
These became part of that child who went forth every day, and who
    now goes and will always go forth every day.

Crossing Brooklyn Ferry

1

Flood-tide below me! I see you, face to face!
Clouds of the west! sun there half an hour high! I see you also face to
    face.

Crowds of men and women attired in the usual costumes! how
    curious you are to me!
On the ferry-boats, the hundreds and hundreds that cross, returning
    home, are more curious to me than you suppose,
And you that shall cross from shore to shore years hence, are more
    to me, and more in my meditations, than you might suppose.

2

The impalpable sustenance of me from all things, at all hours of the
    day,
The simple, compact, well-joined scheme—myself disintegrated,
    every one disintegrated, yet part of the scheme,
The similitudes of the past, and those of the future,
The glories strung like beads on my smallest sights and hearings—on
    the walk in the street, and the passage over the river,
The current rushing so swiftly, and swimming with me far away,
The others that are to follow me, the ties between me and them,
The certainty of others—the life, love, sight, hearing of others.

Others will enter the gates of the ferry, and cross from shore to shore,
Others will watch the run of the flood-tide,
Others will see the shipping of Manhattan north and west, and the
    heights of Brooklyn to the south and east,
Others will see the islands large and small,
Fifty years hence, others will see them as they cross, the sun half an
    hour high,

A hundred years hence, or ever so many hundred years hence,
    others will see them,
Will enjoy the sunset, the pouring-in of the flood-tide, the falling-
    back to the sea of the ebb-tide.

3

It avails not, neither time or place—distance avails not,
I am with you, you men and women of a generation, or ever so many
    generations hence,
Just as you feel when you look on the river and sky, so I felt,
Just as any of you is one of a living crowd, I was one of a crowd,
Just as you are refreshed by the gladness of the river, and the bright
    flow, I was refreshed,
Just as you stand and lean on the rail, yet hurry with the swift current,
    I stood, yet was hurried,
Just as you look on the numberless masts of ships, and the
    thick-stemmed pipes of steamboats, I looked.

I too many and many a time crossed the river of old,
Watched the December sea-gulls—saw them high in the air, floating
    with motionless wings, oscillating their bodies,
Saw how the glistening yellow lit up parts of their bodies, and left the
    rest in strong shadow,
Saw the slow-wheeling circles, and the gradual edging toward the
    south,
Saw the reflection of the summer sky in the water,
Had my eyes dazzled by the shimmering track of beams,
Looked at the fine centrifugal spokes of light round the shape of
    my head in the sunlit water,
Looked on the haze on the hills southward and south-westward,
Looked on the vapor as it flew in fleeces tinged with violet,
Looked toward the lower bay to notice the arriving ships,
Saw their approach, saw aboard those that were near me,
Saw the white sails of schooners and sloops, saw the ships at anchor,

The sailors at work in the rigging, or out astride the spars,
The round masts, the swinging motion of the hulls, the slender
    serpentine pennants,
The large and small steamers in motion, the pilots in their pilot-houses,
The white wake left by the passage, the quick tremulous whirl of the
    wheels,
The flags of all nations, the falling of them at sunset,
The scallop-edged waves in the twilight, the ladled cups, the frolicsome
    crests and glistening,
The stretch afar growing dimmer and dimmer, the gray walls of the
    granite storehouses by the docks,
On the river the shadowy group, the big steam-tug closely flanked
    on each side by the barges—the hay-boat, the belated lighter,
On the neighboring shore, the fires from the foundry chimneys
    burning high and glaringly into the night,
Casting their flicker of black, contrasted with wild red and yellow
    light, over the tops of houses, and down into the clefts of streets.

4
These, and all else, were to me the same as they are to you,
I loved well those cities,
I loved well the stately and rapid river,
The men and women I saw were all near to me,
Others the same—others who look back on me, because I looked
    forward to them,
(The time will come, though I stop here to-day and to-night.)

5
What is it, then, between us?
What is the count of the scores or hundreds of years between us?

Whatever it is, it avails not—distance avails not, and place avails not.

I too lived, Brooklyn of ample hills was mine,

I too walked the streets of Manhattan island, and bathed in the waters
    around it,
I too felt the curious abrupt questionings stir within me,
In the day, among crowds of people, sometimes they came upon me,
In my walks home late at night, or as I lay in my bed, they came
    upon me,
I too had been struck from the float forever held in solution,
I too had received identity by my body,
That I was, I knew was of my body—and what I should be, I knew
    I should be of my body.

6

It is not upon you alone the dark patches fall,
The dark threw patches down upon me also,
The best I had done seemed to me blank and suspicious,
My great thoughts, as I supposed them, were they not in reality
    meagre?
Nor is it you alone who know what it is to be evil,
I am he who knew what it was to be evil,
I too knitted the old knot of contrariety,
Blabbed, blushed, resented, lied, stole, grudged,
Had guile, anger, lust, hot wishes I dared not speak,
Was wayward, vain, greedy, shallow, sly, a solitary committer,
    a coward, a malignant person,
The wolf, the snake, the hog, not wanting in me,
The cheating look, the frivolous word, the adulterous wish, not
    wanting,
Refusals, hates, postponements, meanness, laziness, none of these
    wanting,
Was one with the rest, the days and haps of the rest,
Was called by my nighest name by clear loud voices of young men
    as they saw me approaching or passing,
Felt their arms on my neck as I stood, or the negligent leaning of
    their flesh against me as I sat,

Saw many I loved in the street, or ferry-boat, or public assembly,
　　yet never told them a word,
Lived the same life with the rest, the same old laughing, gnawing,
　　sleeping,
Played the part that still looks back on the actor or actress,
The same old role, the role that is what we make it, as great as
　　we like,
Or as small as we like, or both great and small.

7

Closer yet I approach you,
What thought you have of me, I had as much of you—I laid in
　　my stores in advance,
I considered long and seriously of you before you were born.

Who was to know what should come home to me?
Who knows but I am enjoying this?
Who knows, for all the distance, but I am as good as looking at you
　　now, for all you cannot see me?

8

Ah, what can ever be more stately and admirable to me than my
　　mast-hemm'd Manhattan,
My river and sunset, and my scallop-edged waves of flood-tide,
The sea-gulls oscillating their bodies, the hay-boat in the twilight,
　　and the belated lighter;
What gods can exceed these that clasp me by the hand, and with
　　voices I love call me promptly and loudly by my nighest name
　　as I approach?
What is more subtle than this which ties me to the woman or man
　　that looks in my face,
Which fuses me into you now, and pours my meaning into you?

We understand, then, do we not?

What I promised without mentioning it, have you not accepted?
What the study could not teach—what the preaching could not
  accomplish is accomplished, is it not?

9

Flow on, river! flow with the flood-tide, and ebb with the ebb-tide!
Frolic on, crested and scallop-edged waves!
Gorgeous clouds of the sunset! drench with your splendor me, or
  the men and women generations after me!
Cross from shore to shore, countless crowds of passengers!
Stand up, tall masts of Mannahatta!—stand up, beautiful hills of
  Brooklyn!
Throb, baffled and curious brain! throw out questions and answers!
Suspend here and everywhere, eternal float of solution!
Blab, blush, lie, steal, you or I or any one after us!
Gaze, loving and thirsting eyes, in the house, or street, or public
  assembly!
Sound out, voices of young men! loudly and musically call me by
  my nighest name!
Live, old life! play the part that looks back on the actor or actress!
Play the old role, the role that is great or small, according as one
  makes it!
Consider, you who peruse me, whether I may not in unknown ways
  be looking upon you!
Be firm, rail over the river, to support those who lean idly, yet haste
  with the hasting current!
Fly on, sea-birds! fly sideways, or wheel in large circles high in the air!
Receive the summer-sky, you water! and faithfully hold it, till all
  downcast eyes have time to take it from you!
Diverge, fine spokes of light, from the shape of my head, or any one's
  head, in the sun-lit water!
Come on, ships from the lower bay! pass up or down, white-sailed
  schooners, sloops, lighters!
Flaunt away, flags of all nations! be duly lowered at sunset!

Burn high your fires, foundry chimneys! cast black shadows at
    nightfall! cast red and yellow light over the tops of the houses!
Appearances, now or henceforth, indicate what you are,
You necessary film, continue to envelop the soul,
About my body for me, and your body for you, be hung our
    divinest aromas,
Thrive, cities! bring your freight, bring your shows, ample and
    sufficient rivers,
Expand, being than which none else is perhaps more spiritual,
Keep your places, objects than which none else is more lasting.

You have waited, you always wait, you dumb, beautiful ministers,
We receive you with free sense at last, and are insatiate henceforward,
Not you any more shall be able to foil us, or withhold yourselves
    from us,
We use you, and do not cast you aside—we plant you permanently
    within us,
We fathom you not—we love you—there is perfection in you also,
You furnish your parts toward eternity,
Great or small, you furnish your parts toward the soul.

Poem of the Proposition of Nakedness

Respondez! Respondez!
Let every one answer! let those who sleep be waked! let none evade!
Must we still go on with our affectations and sneaking?
Let me bring this to a close—I pronounce openly for a new distribution
    of roles,
Let that which stood in front go behind! and let that which was behind
    advance to the front and speak!
Let murderers, thieves, bigots, fools, unclean persons, offer new
    propositions!
Let the old propositions be postponed!

Let faces and theories be turned inside out! let meanings be freely
    criminal, as well as results! (Say! can results be criminal, and
    meanings not criminal?)
Let there be no suggestion above the suggestion of drudgery!
Let none be pointed toward his destination! (Say! do you know
    your destination?)
Let men and women be mocked with bodies and mocked with souls!
Let the love that waits in them, wait! let it die, or pass still-born to
    other spheres!
Let the sympathy that waits in every man, wait! or let it also pass,
    a dwarf, to other spheres!
Let contradictions prevail! let one thing contradict another! and let
    one line of my poems contradict another!
Let the people sprawl with yearning aimless hands! let their tongues
    be broken! let their eyes be discouraged! let none descend into
    their hearts with the fresh lusciousness of love!
Let the theory of America be management, caste, comparison! (Say!
    what other theory would you?)
Let them that distrust birth and death lead the rest! (Say! why shall
    they not lead you?)
Let the crust of hell be neared and trod on! let the days be darker than
    the nights! let slumber bring less slumber than waking-time
    brings!
Let the world never appear to him or her for whom it was all made!
Let the heart of the young man exile itself from the heart of the old
    man! and let the heart of the old man be exiled from that of the
    young man!
Let the sun and moon go! let scenery take the applause of the audience!
    let there be apathy under the stars!
Let freedom prove no man's inalienable right! every one who can
    tyrannize, let him tyrannize to his satisfaction!
Let none but infidels be countenanced!
Let the eminence of meanness, treachery, sarcasm, hate, greed,
    indecency, impotence, lust, be taken for granted above all!

let writers, judges, governments, households, religions,
philosophies, take such for granted above all!
Let the worst men beget children out of the worst women!
Let priests still play at immortality!
Let Death be inaugurated!
Let nothing remain upon the earth except the ashes of teachers,
artists, moralists, lawyers, and learned and polite persons!
Let him who is without my poems be assassinated!
Let the cow, the horse, the camel, the garden-bee—let the mud-fish,
the lobster, the mussel, eel, the sting-ray, and the grunting
pig-fish—let these, and the like of these, be put on a perfect
equality with man and woman!
Let churches accommodate serpents, vermin, and the corpses of those
who have died of the most filthy of diseases!
Let marriage slip down among fools, and be for none but fools!
Let men among themselves talk and think obscenely of women! and
let women among themselves talk and think obscenely of men!
Let every man doubt every woman! and let every woman trick every
man!
Let us all, without missing one, be exposed in public naked, monthly,
at the peril of our lives! let our bodies be freely handled and
examined by whoever chooses!
Let nothing but copies at second hand be permitted to exist upon the
earth!
Let the earth desert God, nor let there ever henceforth be mentioned
the name of God!
Let there be no God!
Let there be money, business, imports, exports, custom, authority,
precedents, pallor, dyspepsia, smut, ignorance, unbelief!
Let judges and criminals be transposed! let the prison-keepers be put
in prison! let those that were prisoners take the keys! (Say! why
might they not just as well be transposed?)
Let the slaves be masters! Let the masters become slaves!
Let the reformers descend from the stands where they are forever

bawling! let an idiot or insane person appear on each of the stands!

Let the Asiatic, the African, the European, the American and the Australian, go armed against the murderous stealthiness of each other! let them sleep armed! let none believe in good-will!

Let there be no living wisdom! let such be scorned and derided off from the earth!

Let a floating cloud in the sky—let a wave of the sea—let one glimpse of your eye-sight upon the landscape or grass—let growing mint, spinach, onions, tomatoes—let these be exhibited as shows at a great price for admission!

Let all the men of These States stand aside for a few smouchers! let the few seize on what they choose! let the rest gawk, giggle, starve, obey!

Let shadows be furnished with genitals! let substances be deprived of their genitals!

Let there be wealthy and immense cities—but through any of them, not a single poet, saviour, knower, lover!

Let the infidels of These States laugh all faith away! if one man be found who has faith, let the rest set upon him! let them affright faith! let them destroy the power of breeding faith!

Let the she-harlots and the he-harlots be prudent! Let them dance on, while seeming lasts! (O seeming! seeming! seeming!)

Let the preachers recite creeds! Let them still teach only what they have been taught!

Let the preacher of creeds never dare to go meditate upon the hills, alone, by day or by night! (If one ever once dare, he is lost!)

Let insanity have charge of sanity!

Let books take the place of trees, animals, rivers, clouds!

Let the daubed portraits of heroes supersede heroes!

Let the manhood of man never take steps after itself! let it take steps after eunuchs, and after consumptive and genteel persons!

Let the white person tread the black person under his heel! (Say! which is trodden under heel, after all?)

Let the reflections of the things of the world be studied in mirrors!
    let the things themselves continue unstudied!
Let a man seek pleasure everywhere except in himself! let a woman
    seek happiness everywhere except in herself! (What real happiness
    have you had one single hour through your whole life?)
Let the limited years of life do nothing for the limitless years of death!
    (What do you suppose death will do, then?)

Out of the Cradle Endlessly Rocking

Out of the cradle endlessly rocking,
Out of the mocking-bird's throat, the musical shuttle,
Out of the Ninth-month midnight,
Over the sterile sands, and the fields beyond, where the child,
    leaving his bed, wandered alone, bareheaded, barefoot,
Down from the showered halo,
Up from the mystic play of shadows, twining and twisting as if
    they were alive,
Out from the patches of briers and blackberries,
From the memories of the bird that chanted to me,
From your memories, sad brother—from the fitful risings and
    fallings I heard,
From under that yellow half-moon, late-risen, and swollen as if with
    tears,
From those beginning notes of sickness and love, there in the
    transparent mist,
From the thousand responses of my heart, never to cease,
From the myriad thence-aroused words,
From the word stronger and more delicious than any,
From such, as now they start, the scene revisiting,
As a flock, twittering, rising, or overhead passing,
Borne hither—ere all eludes me, hurriedly,

A man—yet by these tears a little boy again,
Throwing myself on the sand, confronting the waves,
I, chanter of pains and joys, uniter of here and hereafter,
Taking all hints to use them—but swiftly leaping beyond them,
A reminiscence sing.

Once, Paumanok,
When the snows had melted—when the lilac-scent was in the air,
    and the Fifth-month grass was growing,
Up this seashore, in some briers,
Two guests from Alabama—two together,
And their nest, and four light-green eggs, spotted with brown,
And every day the he-bird, to and fro, near at hand,
And every day the she-bird, crouched on her nest, silent, with bright
    eyes,
And every day I, a curious boy, never too close, never disturbing them,
Cautiously peering, absorbing, translating.

Shine! shine!
Pour down your warmth, great sun!
While we bask—we two together.

Two together!
Winds blow south, or winds blow north,
Day come white, or night come black,
Home, or rivers and mountains from home,
Singing all time, minding no time,
If we two but keep together.

Till of a sudden,
May-be killed, unknown to her mate,
One forenoon the she-bird crouched not on the nest,
Nor returned that afternoon, nor the next,
Nor ever appeared again.

And thenceforward, all summer, in the sound of the sea,
And at night, under the full of the moon, in calmer weather,
Over the hoarse surging of the sea,
Or flitting from brier to brier by day,
I saw, I heard at intervals, the remaining one, the he-bird,
The solitary guest from Alabama.

Blow! blow!
Blow up sea-winds along Paumanok's shore;
I wait and I wait, till you blow my mate to me.

Yes, when the stars glistened,
All night long, on the prong of a moss-scallop'd stake,
Down, almost amid the slapping waves,
Sat the lone singer, wonderful, causing tears.

He called on his mate,
He poured forth the meanings which I, of all men, know.

Yes, my brother, I know,
The rest might not—but I have treasured every note,
For once, and more than once, dimly, down to the beach gliding,
Silent, avoiding the moonbeams, blending myself with the shadows,
Recalling now the obscure shapes, the echoes, the sounds and sights
     after their sorts,
The white arms out in the breakers tirelessly tossing,
I, with bare feet, a child, the wind wafting my hair,
Listened long and long.

Listened, to keep, to sing—now translating the notes,
Following you, my brother.

Soothe! soothe!
Close on its wave soothes the wave behind,

And again another behind, embracing and lapping, every one close,
But my love soothes not me.

Low hangs the moon—it rose late,
O it is lagging—O I think it is heavy with love.

O madly the sea pushes upon the land,
With love—with love.

O night! O do I not see my love fluttering out there among the breakers?
What is that little black thing I see there in the white?

Loud! loud!
Loud I call to you my love!
High and clear I shoot my voice over the waves,
Surely you must know who is here,
You must know who I am, my love.

Low-hanging moon!
What is that dusky spot in your brown yellow?
O it is the shape of my mate!
O moon, do not keep her from me any longer.

Land! O land!
Whichever way I turn, O I think you could give me my mate back again,
*   if you would,*
For I am almost sure I see her dimly whichever way I look.

O rising stars!
Perhaps the one I want so much will rise with some of you.

O throat!
Sound clearer through the atmosphere!

Pierce the woods, the earth,
Somewhere listening to catch you must be the one I want.

Shake out, carols!
Solitary here—the night's carols!
Carols of lonesome love! death's carols!
Carols under that lagging, yellow, waning moon!
O under that moon, where she droops almost down into the sea!
O reckless, despairing carols.

But soft! sink low—soft!
Soft! let me just murmur,
And do you wait a moment, you husky-noised sea,
For somewhere I believe I heard my mate responding to me,
So faint—I must be still to listen,
But not altogether still, for then she might not come immediately to me.

Hither, my love!
Here I am! here!
With this just-sustained note I announce myself to you,
This gentle call is for you, my love.

Do not be decoyed elsewhere!
That is the whistle of the wind—it is not my voice,
That is the fluttering of the spray,
Those are the shadows of leaves.

O darkness! O in vain!
O I am very sick and sorrowful.

O brown halo in the sky, near the moon, drooping upon the sea!
O troubled reflection in the sea!
O throat! O throbbing heart!
O all—and I singing uselessly all the night.

Murmur! murmur on!
O murmurs—you yourselves make me continue to sing, I know not why.
O past! O joy!
In the air—in the woods—over fields,
Loved! loved! loved! loved! loved!
Loved—but no more with me,
We two together no more.

The aria sinking,
All else continuing—the stars shining,
The winds blowing—the notes of the wondrous bird echoing,
With angry moans the fierce old mother yet, as ever, incessantly
    moaning,
On the sands of Paumanok's shore gray and rustling,
The yellow half-moon, enlarged, sagging down, drooping, the face
    of the sea almost touching,
The boy ecstatic—with his bare feet the waves, with his hair the
    atmosphere dallying,
The love in the heart pent, now loose, now at last tumultuously
    bursting,
The aria's meaning, the ears, the soul, swiftly depositing,
The strange tears down the cheeks coursing,
The colloquy there—the trio—each uttering,
The undertone—the savage old mother, incessantly crying,
To the boy's soul's questions sullenly timing—some drowned secret
    hissing,
To the outsetting bard of love.

Bird! (then said the boy's soul,)
Is it indeed toward your mate you sing? or is it mostly to me?
For I that was a child, my tongue's use sleeping, now that I have
    heard you,
Now in a moment I know what I am for—I awake,

And already a thousand singers—a thousand songs, clearer, louder,
    more sorrowful than yours,
A thousand warbling echoes have started to life within me,
    never to die.

O throes!
O you demon, singing by yourself—projecting me,
O solitary me, listening—never more shall I cease imitating,
    perpetuating you,
Never more shall I escape, never more shall the reverberations,
Never more the cries of unsatisfied love be absent from me,
Never again leave me to be the peaceful child I was before what there,
    in the night,
By the sea, under the yellow and sagging moon,
The dusky demon aroused—the fire, the sweet hell within,
The unknown want, the destiny of me.

O give me some clew!
O if I am to have so much, let me have more!
O a word! O what is my destination?
I fear it is henceforth chaos!
O how joys, dreads, convolutions, human shapes, and all shapes,
    spring as from graves around me!
O phantoms! you cover all the land, and all the sea!
O I cannot see in the dimness whether you smile or frown upon me;
O vapor, a look, a word! O well-beloved!
O you dear women's and men's phantoms!

A word then, (for I will conquer it,)
The word final, superior to all,
Subtle, sent up—what is it?—I listen;
Are you whispering it, and have been all the time, you sea-waves?
Is that it from your liquid rims and wet sands?

Answering, the sea,
Delaying not, hurrying not,
Whispered me through the night, and very plainly before daybreak,
Lisped to me constantly the low and delicious word death,
And again death—death, death, death,
Hissing melodious, neither like the bird, nor like my aroused child's
  heart,
But edging near, as privately for me, rustling at my feet,
And creeping thence steadily up to my ears,
Death, death, death, death, death.

Which I do not forget,
But fuse the song of two together,
That was sung to me in the moonlight on Paumanok's gray beach,
With the thousand responsive songs, at random,
My own songs, awaked from that hour,
And with them the key, the word up from the waves,
The word of the sweetest song, and all songs,
That strong and delicious word which, creeping to my feet,
The sea whispered me.

Elemental Drifts

1

As I ebbed with the ocean of life,
As I wended the shores I know,
As I walked where the sea-ripples wash you, Paumanok,
Where they rustle up, hoarse and sibilant,
Where the fierce old mother endlessly cries for her castaways,
I, musing, late in the autumn day, gazing off southward,
Alone, held by the eternal self of me that threatens to get the better
  of me, and stifle me,
Was seized by the spirit that trails in the lines underfoot,

In the rim, the sediment, that stands for all the water and all the land
    of the globe.

Fascinated, my eyes, reverting from the south, dropped, to follow
    those slender windrows,
Chaff, straw, splinters of wood, weeds, and the sea-gluten,
Scum, scales from shining rocks, leaves of salt-lettuce, left by the tide,
Miles walking, the sound of breaking waves the other side of me,
Paumanok, there and then, as I thought the old thought of likenesses,
These you presented to me, you fish-shaped island,
As I wended the shores I know,
As I walked with that eternal self of me, seeking types.

2
As I wend the shores I know not,
As I listen to the dirge, the voices of men and women wrecked,
As I inhale the impalpable breezes that set in upon me,
As the ocean so mysterious rolls toward me closer and closer,
At once I find, the least thing that belongs to me, or that I see or touch,
    I know not,
I, too, but signify, at the utmost, a little washed-up drift,
A few sands and dead leaves to gather,
Gather, and merge, myself as part of the sands and drift.

O baffled, balked,
Bent to the very earth, here preceding what follows,
Oppressed with myself that I have dared to open my mouth,
Aware now, that, amid all the blab whose echoes recoil upon me,
    I have not once had the least idea who or what I am,
But that before all my insolent poems the real Me still stands
    untouched, untold, altogether unreached,
Withdrawn far, mocking me with mock-congratulatory signs and
    bows,

With peals of distant ironical laughter at every word I have written
    or shall write,
Striking me with insults till I fall helpless upon the sand.

O I perceive I have not understood anything—not a single object—
    and that no man ever can.

I perceive Nature here, in sight of the sea, is taking advantage of me,
    to dart upon me, and sting me,
Because I was assuming so much,
And because I have dared to open my mouth to sing at all.

3
You oceans both! You tangible land! Nature!
Be not too rough with me—I submit—I close with you,
These little shreds shall, indeed, stand for all.

You friable shore, with trails of debris!
You fish-shaped island! I take what is underfoot,
What is yours is mine, my father.

I too Paumanok,
I too have bubbled up, floated the measureless float, and been
    washed on your shores,
I too am but a trail of drift and debris,
I too leave little wrecks upon you, you fish-shaped island.

I throw myself upon your breast, my father,
I cling to you so that you cannot unloose me,
I hold you so firm, till you answer me something.

Kiss me, my father,
Touch me with your lips, as I touch those I love,

Breathe to me, while I hold you close, the secret of the wondrous
    murmuring I envy,
For I fear I shall become crazed, if I cannot emulate it, and utter
    myself as well as it.

Sea-raff! Crook-tongued waves!
O I will yet sing, some day, what you have said to me.

4

Ebb, ocean of life, (the flow will return,)
Cease not your moaning, you fierce old mother,
Endlessly cry for your castaways—but fear not, deny not me,
Rustle not up so hoarse and angry against my feet, as I touch you,
    or gather from you.

I mean tenderly by you,
I gather for myself, and for this phantom, looking down where we
    lead, and following me and mine.

Me and mine!
We, loose windrows, little corpses,
Froth, snowy white, and bubbles,
(See! from my dead lips the ooze exuding at last!
See—the prismatic colors, glistening and rolling!)
Tufts of straw, sands, fragments,
Buoyed hither from many moods, one contradicting another,
From the storm, the long calm, the darkness, the swell,
Musing, pondering, a breath, a briny tear, a dab of liquid or soil,
Up just as much out of fathomless workings fermented and thrown,
A limp blossom or two, torn, just as much over waves floating,
    drifted at random,
Just as much for us that sobbing dirge of Nature,
Just as much, whence we come, that blare of the cloud-trumpets,

We, capricious, brought hither, we know not whence, spread out
    before you, up there, walking or sitting,
Whoever you are—we too lie in drifts at your feet.

Once I Passed Through a Populous City

Once I passed through a populous city, imprinting on my brain, for
    future use, its shows, architecture, customs and traditions
But now of all that city I remember only the man who wandered with
    me there, for love of me,
Day by day, and night by night, we were together.
All else has long been forgotten by me—I remember, I say, only one
    rude and ignorant man who, when I departed, long and long held
    me by the hand, with silent lips, sad and tremulous.

When I Heard at the Close of the Day

When I heard at the close of the day how my name had been received
    with plaudits in the capitol, still it was not a happy night for me
    that followed,
And else, when I caroused, or when my plans were accomplished, still
    I was not happy,
But the day when I rose at dawn from the bed of perfect health,
    refreshed, singing, inhaling the ripe breath of autumn,
When I saw the full moon in the west grow pale and disappear in
    the morning light,
When I wandered alone over the beach, and, undressing, bathed,
    laughing with the cool waters, and saw the sun rise,
And when I thought how my dear friend, my lover, was on his way
    coming, O then I was happy,
O then each breath tasted sweeter—and all that day my food nourished
    me more—and the beautiful day passed well,

And the next came with equal joy—and with the next, at evening,
    came my friend,
And that night, while all was still, I heard the waters roll slowly
    continually up the shores,
I heard the hissing rustle of the liquid and sands, as directed to me,
    whispering, to congratulate me,
For the one I love most lay sleeping by me under the same cover in
    the cool night,
In the stillness, in the autumn moonbeams, his face was inclined
    toward me,
And his arm lay lightly around my breast—and that night I was happy.

A Glimpse

A glimpse, through an interstice caught,
Of a crowd of workmen and drivers in a bar-room, around the stove,
    late of a winter night—and I unremarked, seated in a corner,
Of a youth who loves me, and whom I love, silently approaching, and
    seating himself near, that he may hold me by the hand,
A long while, amid the noises of coming and going—of drinking and
    oath and smutty jest,
There we two, content, happy in being together, speaking little, perhaps
    not a word.

The Runner

On a flat road runs the well-train'd runner,
He is lean and sinewy, with muscular legs,
He is thinly clothed—he leans forward as he runs,
With lightly closed fists, and arms partially rais'd.

Sparkles from the Wheel

Where the city's ceaseless crowd moves on the livelong day,
Withdrawn I join a group of children watching—I pause aside with
    them.

By the curb toward the edge of the flagging,
A knife-grinder works at his wheel sharpening a great knife,
Bending over he carefully holds it to the stone—by foot and knee,
With measur'd tread he turns rapidly—as he presses with light but
    firm hand,
Forth issue then in copious golden jets,
Sparkles from the wheel.

The scene and all its belongings—how they seize and affect me,
The sad sharp-chinn'd old man with worn clothes and broad shoulder-
    band of leather,
Myself effusing and fluid—a phantom curiously floating—now here
    absorb'd and arrested,
The group, (an unminded point set in a vast surrounding,)
The attentive, quiet children—the loud, proud, restive bass of the streets,
The low hoarse purr of the whirling stone, the light-press'd blade,
Diffusing, dropping, sideways-darting, in tiny showers of gold,
Sparkles from the wheel.

Bivouac on a Mountain Side

I see before me now, a traveling army halting,
Below, a fertile valley spread, with barns, and the orchards of summer,
Behind, the terraced sides of a mountain, abrupt in places, rising high,
Broken, with rocks, with clinging cedars, with tall shapes, dingily seen,
The numerous camp-fires scatter'd near and far, some away up on the
    mountain,

The shadowy forms of men and horses, looming, large-sized, flickering,
And over all, the sky—the sky! far, far out of reach, studded with the
    eternal stars.

Vigil Strange I Kept on the Field One Night

Vigil strange I kept on the field one night,
When you, my son and my comrade, dropt at my side that day,
One look I but gave, which your dear eyes return'd, with a look I shall
    never forget,
One touch of your hand to mine, O boy, reach'd up as you lay on the
    ground,
Then onward I sped in the battle, the even-contested battle,
Till late in the night reliev'd, to the place at last again I made my way,
Found you in death so cold, dear comrade—found your body, son of
    responding kisses, (never again on earth responding,)
Bared your face in the starlight—curious the scene—cool blew the
    moderate night-wind,
Long there and then in vigil I stood, dimly around me the battle-field
    spreading,
Vigil wondrous and vigil sweet, there in the fragrant silent night,
But not a tear fell, not even a long-drawn sigh—long, long I gazed,
Then on the earth partially reclining, sat by your side, leaning my chin
    in my hands,
Passing sweet hours, immortal and mystic hours with you, dearest
    comrade—not a tear, not a word,
Vigil of silence, love and death—vigil for you my son and my soldier,
As onward silently stars aloft, eastward new ones upward stole,
Vigil final for you, brave boy, (I could not save you, swift was your
    death,
I faithfully loved you and cared for you living—I think we shall surely
    meet again,)
Till at latest lingering of the night, indeed just as the dawn appear'd,

My comrade I wrapt in his blanket, envelop'd well his form,
Folded the blanket well, tucking it carefully over head, and carefully
    under feet,
And there and then, and bathed by the rising sun, my son in his grave,
    in his rude-dug grave I deposited,
Ending my vigil strange with that—vigil of night and battle-field dim,
Vigil for boy of responding kisses, (never again on earth responding,)
Vigil for comrade swiftly slain—vigil I never forget, how as day
    brighten'd,
I rose from the chill ground, and folded my soldier well in his blanket,
And buried him where he fell.

Reconciliation

Word over all, beautiful as the sky,
Beautiful that war and all its deeds of carnage must in time be utterly
    lost,
That the hands of the sisters Death and Night incessantly softly wash
    again, and ever again, this soil'd world;
For my enemy is dead, a man divine as myself is dead,
I look where he lies white-faced and still in the coffin—I draw near,
Bend down and touch lightly with my lips the white face in the coffin.

When Lilacs Last in the Door-yard Bloom'd

1

When lilacs last in the door-yard bloom'd,
And the great star early droop'd in the western sky in the night,
I mourn'd—and yet shall mourn with ever-returning spring.

O ever-returning spring! trinity sure to me you bring,
Lilac blooming perennial, and drooping star in the west,
And thought of him I love.

2

O powerful, western, fallen star!
O shades of night! O moody, tearful night!
O great star disappear'd! O the black murk that hides the star!
O cruel hands that hold me powerless! O helpless soul of me!
O harsh surrounding cloud, that will not free my soul!

3

In the door-yard fronting an old farm-house, near the whitewash'd
    palings,
Stands the lilac bush, tall-growing, with heart-shaped leaves of rich
    green,
With many a pointed blossom, rising, delicate, with the perfume
    strong I love,
With every leaf a miracle—and from this bush in the door-yard,
With delicate-color'd blossoms, and heart-shaped leaves of rich green,
A sprig, with its flower, I break.

4

In the swamp, in secluded recesses,
A shy and hidden bird is warbling a song.

Solitary, the thrush,
The hermit, withdrawn to himself, avoiding the settlements,
Sings by himself a song.

Song of the bleeding throat,
Death's outlet song of life—(for well, dear brother, I know
If thou wast not gifted to sing, thou would'st surely die.)

5

Over the breast of the spring, the land, amid cities,
Amid lanes, and through old woods, (where lately the violets peep'd
    from the ground, spotting the gray debris,)

Amid the grass in the fields each side of the lanes—passing the
    endless grass,
Passing the yellow-spear'd wheat, every grain from its shroud in the
    dark-brown fields uprisen,
Passing the apple-tree blows of white and pink in the orchards,
Carrying a corpse to where it shall rest in the grave,
Night and day journeys a coffin.

6

Coffin that passes through lanes and streets,
Through day and night, with the great cloud darkening the land,
With the pomp of the inloop'd flags, with the cities draped in black,
With the show of the States themselves, as of crape-veil'd women,
    standing,
With processions long and winding, and the flambeaus of the night,
With the countless torches lit—with the silent sea of faces, and the
    unbared heads,
With the waiting depot, the arriving coffin, and the sombre faces,
With dirges through the night, with the thousand voices rising strong
    and solemn,
With all the mournful voices of the dirges, pour'd around the coffin,
The dim-lit churches and the shuddering organs—where amid these
    you journey,
With the tolling, tolling bells' perpetual clang,
Here! coffin that slowly passes,
I give you my sprig of lilac.

7

(Nor for you, for one, alone,
Blossoms and branches green to coffins all I bring,
For fresh as the morning—thus would I carol a song for you, O sane
    and sacred death.

All over bouquets of roses,
O death, I cover you over with roses and early lilies,
But mostly and now the lilac that blooms the first,
Copious, I break, I break the sprigs from the bushes,
With loaded arms I come, pouring for you,
For you, and the coffins all of you, O death.)

8

O western orb, sailing the heaven,
Now I know what you must have meant, as a month since we walk'd,
As we walk'd up and down in the dark blue so mystic,
As we walk'd in silence the transparent shadowy night,
As I saw you had something to tell, as you bent to me night after night,
As you droop'd from the sky low down, as if to my side, (while the
    other stars all look'd on,)
As we wander'd together the solemn night, (for something, I know not
    what, kept me from sleep,)
As the night advanced, and I saw on the rim of the west, ere you went,
    how full you were of woe,
As I stood on the rising ground in the breeze, in the cold transparent
    night,
As I watch'd where you pass'd and was lost in the netherward black
    of the night,
As my soul, in its trouble, dissatisfied, sank, as where you, sad orb,
Concluded, dropt in the night, and was gone.

9

Sing on, there in the swamp!
O singer bashful and tender! I hear your notes—I hear your call,
I hear—I come presently—I understand you,
But a moment I linger—for the lustrous star has detain'd me,
The star, my comrade departing, holds and detains me.

10

O how shall I warble myself for the dead one there I loved?
And how shall I deck my song for the large sweet soul that has gone?
And what shall my perfume be, for the grave of him I love?

Sea-winds, blown from east and west,
Blown from the eastern sea, and blown from the western sea, till there
    on the prairies meeting,
These, and with these, and the breath of my chant,
I perfume the grave of him I love.

11

O what shall I hang on the chamber walls?
And what shall the pictures be that I hang on the walls,
To adorn the burial-house of him I love?

Pictures of growing spring, and farms, and homes,
With the Fourth-month eve at sundown, and the gray smoke lucid
    and bright,
With floods of the yellow gold of the gorgeous, indolent, sinking sun,
    burning, expanding the air,
With the fresh sweet herbage under foot, and the pale green leaves of
    the trees prolific,
In the distance the flowing glaze, the breast of the river, with a
    wind-dapple here and there,
With ranging hills on the banks, with many a line against the sky,
    and shadows,
And the city at hand, with dwellings so dense, and stacks of chimneys,
And all the scenes of life, and the workshops, and the workmen
    homeward returning.

12

Lo! body and soul! this land!
Mighty Manhattan, with spires, and the sparkling and hurrying tides,
    and the ships,

The varied and ample land—the South and the North in the light—
    Ohio's shores, and flashing Missouri,
And ever the far-spreading prairies, cover'd with grass and corn.

Lo! the most excellent sun, so calm and haughty,
The violet and purple morn, with just-felt breezes,
The gentle, soft-born, measureless light,
The miracle, spreading, bathing all—the fulfill'd noon,
The coming eve, delicious—the welcome night, and the stars,
Over my cities shining all, enveloping man and land.

13
Sing on! sing on, you gray-brown bird!
Sing from the swamps, the recesses—pour your chant from the bushes,
Limitless out of the dusk, out of the cedars and pines.

Sing on, dearest brother—warble your reedy song,
Loud human song, with voice of uttermost woe.

O liquid, and free, and tender!
O wild and loose to my soul—O wondrous singer!
You only I hear—yet the star holds me, (but will soon depart,)
Yet the lilac, with mastering odor, holds me.

14
Now while I sat in the day, and look'd forth,
In the close of the day, with its light, and the fields of spring, and the
    farmer preparing his crops,
In the large unconscious scenery of my land, with its lakes and forests,
In the heavenly aerial beauty, (after the perturb'd winds, and the
    storms,)
Under the arching heavens of the afternoon swift passing, and the
    voices of children and women,
The many-moving sea-tides,—and I saw the ships how they sail'd,

And the summer approaching with richness, and the fields all busy
    with labor,
And the infinite separate houses, how they all went on, each with its
    meals and minutia of daily usages,
And the streets, how their throbbings throbb'd, and the cities pent—lo!
    then and there,
Falling among them all, and upon them all, enveloping me with the
    rest,
Appear'd the cloud, appear'd the long black trail,
And I knew death, its thought, and the sacred knowledge of death.

Then with the knowledge of death as walking one side of me,
And the thought of death close-walking the other side of me,
And I in the middle, as with companions, and as holding the hands
    of companions,
I fled forth to the hiding receiving night, that talks not,
Down to the shores of the water, the path by the swamp in the
    dimness,
To the solemn shadowy cedars, and ghostly pines so still.

And the singer so shy to the rest receiv'd me,
The gray-brown bird I know, receiv'd us comrades three,
And he sang what seem'd the song of death, and a verse for him I love.

From deep secluded recesses,
From the fragrant cedars, and the ghostly pines so still,
Came the singing of the bird.

And the charm of the singing rapt me,
As I held, as if by their hands, my comrades in the night,
And the voice of my spirit tallied the song of the bird.

Come, lovely and soothing death,
Undulate round the world, serenely arriving, arriving,

In the day, in the night, to all, to each,
Sooner or later, delicate death.

Prais'd be the fathomless universe,
For life and joy, and for objects and knowledge curious,
And for love, sweet love—but praise! O praise and praise!
For the sure-enwinding arms of cool-enfolding death.

Dark mother, always gliding near, with soft feet,
Have none chanted for thee a chant of fullest welcome?
Then I chant it for thee—I glorify thee above all,
I bring thee a song that when thou must indeed come, come unfalteringly.

Approach, strong deliveress!
When it is so—when thou hast taken them, I joyously sing the dead,
Lost in the loving, floating ocean of thee,
Laved in the flood of thy bliss, O death.

From me to thee glad serenades,
Dances for thee I propose, saluting thee—adornments and feastings for thee,
And the sights of the open landscape, and the high-spread sky, are fitting,
And life and the fields, and the huge and thoughtful night.

The night, in silence, under many a star,
The ocean shore, and the husky whispering wave, whose voice I know,
And the soul turning to thee, O vast and well-veil'd death,
And the body gratefully nestling close to thee.

Over the tree-tops I float thee a song!
Over the rising and sinking waves—over the myriad fields, and the
*   prairies wide,*
Over the dense-pack'd cities all, and the teeming wharves and ways,
I float this carol with joy, with joy to thee, O death!

15

To the tally of my soul,
Loud and strong kept up the gray-brown bird,
With pure, deliberate notes, spreading, filling the night.

Loud in the pines and cedars dim,
Clear in the freshness moist, and the swamp-perfume,
And I with my comrades there in the night.

While my sight that was bound in my eyes unclosed,
As to long panoramas of visions.

And I saw askant the armies,
I saw, as in noiseless dreams, hundreds of battle-flags,
Borne through the smoke of the battles, and pierc'd with missiles,
    I saw them,
And carried hither and yon through the smoke, and torn and bloody,
And at last but a few shreds left on the staffs, (and all in silence,)
And the staffs all splinter'd and broken.

I saw battle-corpses, myriads of them,
And the white skeletons of young men—I saw them,
I saw the debris and debris of all the dead soldiers of the war,
But I saw they were not as was thought,
They themselves were fully at rest—they suffer'd not,
The living remain'd and suffer'd—the mother suffer'd,
And the wife and the child, and the musing comrade suffer'd,
And the armies that remain'd suffer'd.

16

Passing the visions, passing the night,
Passing, unloosing the hold of my comrades' hands,
Passing the song of the hermit bird, and the tallying song of my soul,
Victorious song, death's outlet song, yet varying, ever-altering song,

As low and wailing, yet clear the notes, rising and falling, flooding
    the night,
Sadly sinking and fainting, as warning and warning, and yet again
    bursting with joy,
Covering the earth, and filling the spread of the heaven,
As that powerful psalm in the night I heard from recesses,
Must I leave thee, lilac with heart-shaped leaves,
Must I leave thee there in the door-yard, blooming, returning with
    spring,
Must I pass from my song for thee,
From my gaze on thee in the west, fronting the west, communing
    with thee,
O comrade lustrous, with silver face in the night.

Yet each I keep, and all, retrievements out of the night,
The song, the wondrous chant of the gray-brown bird I keep,
And the tallying chant, the echo arous'd in my soul I keep,
With the lustrous and drooping star, with the countenance full of woe,
With the lilac tall, and its blossoms of mastering odor,
With the holders holding my hand, nearing the call of the bird,
Comrades mine, and I in the midst, and their memory ever I keep—for
    the dead I loved so well,
For the sweetest, wisest soul of all my days and lands—and this for
    his dear sake;
Lilac and star and bird, twined with the chant of my soul,
There in the fragrant pines, and the cedars dusk and dim.

The Last Invocation

At the last, tenderly,
From the walls of the powerful fortress'd house,
From the clasp of the knitted locks, from the keep of the
    well-closed doors,
Let me be wafted.

Let me glide noiselessly forth;
With the key of softness unlock the locks — with a whisper,
Set ope the doors O soul.

Tenderly — be not impatient,
(Strong is your hold O mortal flesh,
Strong is your hold O love.)

✤ ABOUT THE TEXT ✤

Following the title of each poem are the date of the version used in this book; the other titles, if any, under which it appeared; and the section and line numbers where readings from other versions have been incorporated (except when these are limited to punctuation, spelling, and lineation).

Song of Myself: A Poem of Walt Whitman, an American 1855 (1855: without title; 1856: *A Poem of Walt Whitman, an American*; 1860: *Walt Whitman*; 1881: *Song of Myself*) **3.** Line 9: 1856. **5.** Lines 6 and 7: 1860; line 10: 1867; line 12: 1856. **7.** Line after line 14, dropped: 1867. **8.** Line 9: 1856. **15.** Line after line 27, dropped: 1867. **17.** Line after line 2, dropped: 1867. **24.** Line 31: 1867. **32.** Line 8: 1881. **33.** Line 69: 1860. **37.** Line 2: 1860; seven lines after line 2 and two lines after last line, dropped: 1867. **42.** Line 7: 1856. **46.** Line 8: 1860; line 9: 1881; lines 22 and 27: 1867. **51.** Line 3: 1881.

Sleep-Chasings 1855 (1855: without title; 1856: *Night Poem*; 1860: with this title; 1871: *The Sleepers*) **1.** Lines 65 and 66: 1856. **8.** Two lines after last line, dropped: 1856.

Poem of the Body 1881 (1855: without title; 1856: with this title; 1867: *I Sing the Body Electric*) **1.** Lines 3 and 4: 1856. **2.** Lines 16 and 20: 1856. **5.** Line after last line, dropped: 1860. **6.** Line 14: 1881;

lines 15 and 17: 1860. **7.** Line 7: 1856. **9.** Entire section added: 1856; line 2: 1860.

There Was a Child Went Forth 1855 (1855: without title; 1856: *Poem of the Child That Went Forth, and Always Goes Forth, Forever and Forever*; 1871: with this title) Line 2: 1867. Line after last line, dropped: 1867.

Crossing Brooklyn Ferry 1881 (1856: *Sun-Down Poem*; 1860: with this title) **6.** Line 10: 1856. **9.** Line 7: 1856.

Poem of the Proposition of Nakedness 1856 (1856: with this title; 1867: *Respondez!*; excluded from *Leaves of Grass*: 1881) Lines 2 and 3: 1871. Line 4: 1860. Line 11: 1871. Line 27: 1860. Lines 35, 50, 58, and 59: 1871.

Out of the Cradle Endlessly Rocking 1860 (1860: *A Word Out of the Sea*; 1871: with this title) Line 1: 1871. Line after line 2, dropped: 1867. Line 24: 1871.

Elemental Drifts 1860 (1860: without title; 1867: with this title; 1881: *As I Ebbed with the Ocean of Life*) Two lines before first line, dropped: 1881.

Once I Passed Through a Populous City, undated (Manuscript: without title; 1860: without title; 1867: with this title).

When I Heard at the Close of the Day 1860 (1860: without title; 1867: with this title).

A Glimpse 1867 (1860: without title).

The Runner 1867.

Sparkles from the Wheel 1871.

Bivouac on a Mountain Side 1865.

Vigil Strange I Kept on the Field One Night 1865.

Reconciliation 1881 .

When Lilacs Last in the Door-yard Bloom'd 1865–6 **5.** Line 4: 1881; **14.** Line 40: 1871; **15.** Lines 9 and 10: 1881; lines 13 and 17: 1871; **16.** Line 14: 1871; line **19:** 1871; line after line 22, dropped: **1871.**

The Last Invocation (1871).

ABOUT THE EDITOR

Galway Kinnell lives in Vermont and New York City. He has been the director of an adult education program in Chicago, a journalist in Iran, and a field worker for the Congress of Racial Equality in Louisiana. During the past twenty years he has taught at colleges and universities in this country and in France and Australia. His Selected Poems, *published in 1982, won the Pulitzer Prize and, with Charles Wright's* Country Music, *the American Book Award. His most recent book of poems is* The Past. *Galway Kinnell is Samuel F. B. Morse Professor of Arts and Science at New York University, where he teaches creative writing.*